Emmeline Pankhurst

AF202565

Access all the accompanying digital components for this book
on **allango**, the DELTA Publishing language learning platform:

| Scan the QR code or go directly to **www.allango.co.uk** | Search for the title or the ISBN and click on the cover image | Access content, use now or save for later |

When you see this symbol, accompanying digital content is available.

Angela Hill

Emmeline Pankhurst

DELTA Publishing

Images:
6 123RF.com (yupiramos), Nidderau; **7, 93** gemeinfrei; **17, 18** 123RF.com (subjob); **86** Mrs. S. Burgess, CC BY 4.0, via Wikimedia Commons; **92** gemeinfrei; **93** gemeinfrei; **94.1** gemeinfrei; **94.2** gemeinfrei; **94.3** gemeinfrei; **94.4** LSE Library, No restrictions, via Wikimedia Commons; **94.5** gemeinfrei; **96** 123RF.com (Farrukh Maqbool); **106** gemeinfrei; **107.1** LSE Library, No restrictions, via Wikimedia Commons; **107.2** gemeinfrei; **115** Johnny Cyprus, CC BY-SA 3.0, via Wikimedia Commons

1st edition   1 ⁵ ⁴ ³ ² ¹ | 2027 26 25 24 23

Delta Publishing, 2023
www.deltapublishing.co.uk
© Ernst Klett Sprachen GmbH, Rotebühlstraße 77, 70178 Stuttgart, 2023

Author: Angela Hill
Editor: Kate Baade
Cover and layout: Andreas Drabarek, Eva Lettenmayer
Illustrations: Szilvia Szakall, Beehive Illustration
Typesetting: Datagroup Int. SRL, Timisoara, Romania
Cover picture: Szilvia Szakall, Beehive Illustration
Printing and binding: Plump Druck & Medien GmbH, Rheinbreitbach

Printed in Germany
ISBN 978-3-12-501171-7

Contents

Abbreviations
sb   somebody
sth   something

Before you start

Is the country where you live a democracy - in other words, can all adults vote to elect representatives to the national government? Are there any restrictions on who can vote?

When every adult can vote, it is called universal suffrage. Suffrage is the right to vote in political elections. In the UK, universal suffrage for all adults over the age of 21 was introduced in 1928. Before 1918, the right to vote depended on a person owning property and was restricted to men. The first major change to the UK election system was in 1832 when the first Reform Act increased the number of voters to around 650,000 men, 18% of the total adult male population in England and Wales. Over the years, men and women campaigned hard to get the right to vote so they could be represented in their government.

If women can vote in your country, do you know when they were first given the right? Was it at the same time as men or after?

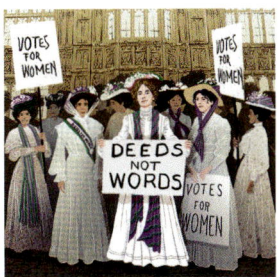

Look at the table on the next page and see if you can match the country to the dates when men and women were able to vote.

Write the letter (a-k) of the date in the space next to the number (1-10) of the country. The first one is done as an example.

Country	Universal male suffrage	Universal female suffrage
1. Argentina	a. 1970	1970
2. Austria	b. 1871	1919
3. Belgium	c. 1999	1999
4. Chile	d. 1853	1952
5. Egypt	e. 1923	1956
6. Finland	f. 1879	1893
7. Germany	g. 1896	1918
8. India	h. 1906	1906
9. New Zealand	i. 1950	1950
10. Qatar	j. 1893	1948

1. _d_ 2. _____ 3. _____ 4. _____ 5._____ 6. _____ 7. _____
8. _____ 9. _____ 10. _____

Now look at the answer key at the back of this book. Which dates surprised you most? Why?

suffragist (noun) - sb who fights for a group of people to have the right to vote in elections
suffrage (noun) – having the right to vote in political elections

Introduction

The timeline

Look at the timeline of events before the story begins (pages 11 to 16) and answer the following questions. The first one has been done as an example.

1. When and where was Emmeline Pankhurst born?
    On 15th July 1858 in Manchester, England

2. How many reform acts were there in the 1800s and what did they do?

3. When did the women's suffrage campaign start?

4. When Emmeline was 14, where did she go?

5. Why was Richard Pankhurst called 'the Red Doctor'?

6. What did Richard Pankhurst do for women's rights?

7. When did Emmeline and Richard get married?

8. How many children did Emmeline have?

9. What did the Poor Law Guardians do?

10. What did Emmeline do when her husband died?

11. What problems did female teachers have in Manchester?

12. What was the WSPU?

13. What happened to the women's suffrage bill in May 1905?

Timeline: Before the story begins

Year	Personal events in Emmeline's life	Political events
1832		**First Reform Act** – votes given to a wider group of men in England and Wales who own or rent property. First petition from a woman asking for the right to vote presented to Parliament. The woman was called Mary Smith and her petition was unsuccessful.
15 July 1858	Emmeline Goulden, is born in Manchester, England	
1866		First women's suffrage mass petition signed by 1,500 women presented in the House of Commons by John Stuart Mill MP. This was the start of an organised campaign for women's suffrage in the UK.
1867		**Second Reform Act** – votes given to more men who own property. Electorate in England and Wales doubles from one to two million men. Encouraged by this reform, many women's suffrage movements are formed including the Manchester National Society for Women's Suffrage (**MNSWS**). Dr Richard Pankhurst is one of the early members of the Executive Committee.

15 **mass** including a large number of people – 19 **campaign** a planned group of political activities intended to achieve an objective – 29 **executive committee** a group of people who manage an organisation

Year	Personal events in Emmeline's life	Political events
1870		**Married Women's Property Act** rules that wages or property earned through a woman's own work or inherited from her family are hers. Before this act, any money made by a woman became the property of her husband when she married.
1872		Emmeline, aged 14, goes to her first suffrage meeting with her mother to hear one of the leaders of the MNSWS talk.
1879	Emmeline meets Dr. Richard Pankhurst in autumn 1878 at a political meeting and in December 1879 they are married. She becomes Mrs Emmeline Pankhurst. She is 21 and Dr Pankhurst is 44.	Dr. Richard Pankhurst is a radical lawyer, who is known in Manchester as 'the Red Doctor' because of his left-wing political views. He has drafted bills and worked on court cases aiming at giving women the vote.
1880	Daughter Christabel is born	Emmeline joins the executive committee of the MNSWS.
1882	Daughter Sylvia is born	Richard Pankhurst drafts a bill which becomes the second **Married Women's Property Act** giving married women complete control over their personal finances and property.

5 **to inherit** to receive money, a house etc from sb who has died – 12 **radical** supporting big political or social change – 14 **left-wing** supporting the ideas of political parties on the left who believe in social equality – 15 **to draft** to write sth that isn't in its finished form yet

Year	Personal events in Emmeline's life	Political events
1884	Son Henry Francis (Frank) is born but dies in 1888 of diphtheria.	**Third Reform Act** – gives vote to more men who rent property. Over 5.5 million men are able to vote. 40% of men and all women are still disenfranchised.
1885	Daughter Adela is born.	Emmeline accompanies and helps her husband campaign to be a member of parliament. He is not successful, but Emmeline gets useful knowledge of how political campaigns work.
1886	The Pankhursts move to London.	Emmeline works with striking female workers at the Bryant and May match factories. The strike is successful and the girl's working conditions are improved a lot.
1889	Second son born and named Henry Francis in honour of Frank who died the previous year.	The Women's Franchise League is formed.
1891		Emmeline joins the Women's Franchise League and starts campaigning in London for women to get the vote.
1893	The Pankhursts return to Manchester.	Emmeline goes back to working at the Women's Suffrage Society.
1894		Emmeline joins the Board of Poor Law Guardians which controls workhouses. Workhouses were places where very poor people who didn't have money to pay for a room could go.

---

6 **diphtheria** a serious infection that affects the nose and throat – 12 **to strike** to refuse to work because you want more money or better conditions – 18 **in honour of** sth done to celebrate sb – 27 **board** group of people who control an organisation

---

Year	Personal events in Emmeline's life	Political events
1894		They got a bed and a small ration of food but everyone, including very old people, ill people, pregnant women, and young children had to work. Emmeline is shocked by the terrible conditions, especially for mothers and their children and old women who had worked all their lives for very low wages and had never been able to save. Emmeline believes that the only way the conditions of these women will be improved is if they can vote. She thinks that men in power do not understand or care about the problems these women face.
1897		The National Union of Women's Suffrage Societies (NUWSS) forms, uniting 17 other suffrage societies. Its most famous leader will be Millicent Fawcett. The NUWSS believe in peaceful campaign methods for example petitions to Parliament.
1898	Dr. Pankhurst dies and Emmeline has to take care of the family. Her oldest daughter, Christabel is 17.	Emmeline finds a job working as a registrar of births and deaths in a working-class area of Manchester. When women come to register the births of their children, many of them tell Emmeline about their experiences and she is again shocked how women and girls are treated. She is more convinced that women need to get the vote so they can use their power to help improve conditions.

3 **ration** a fixed amount of food that you are allowed – 17 **to unite** to join together to make one group – 24 **registrar** sb whose job it is to keep official records

Year	Personal events in Emmeline's life	Political events
1900		Emmeline becomes a member of the Manchester school board. She sees that male teachers earn a higher salary than women, but that the female teachers do more work. The women also often spend their own salaries on providing regular dinners for very poor children. Working on the Committee of the Manchester Technical College, she sees that thousands of pounds are spent on technical training for males but almost nothing is spent on training women.
1903		Emmeline starts the Women's Social and Political Union (**WSPU**). Only women can be members and their political objective is getting the vote. Their motto is '**Deeds, not words.**'
May 1905		The WSPU persuade a Labour MP to introduce a women's suffrage bill in Parliament. The bill is not supported by the Conservative government, who have been in power for nearly 20 years, and they allow it to be 'talked out'. The WSPU organise a demonstration outside Parliament – the first time that suffragists have protested in public. The police take the names of the women giving speeches.

11 **technical college** a place for specialised education after the age of 16 where people study practical subjects – 25 **to talk a bill out** to stop a bill in Parliament from being successful by discussing it for too long – 26 **demonstration** when a group of people stand or walk together in order to protest against or support sth

Year	Personal events in Emmeline's life	Political events
December 1905	Emmeline resigns from her job as a registrar in Manchester and moves to London.	

You can find a political glossary in the **Build your vocabulary** section. Definitions of words highlighted in purple can all be found in this glossary.

---

3 **to resign** to tell your employer officially that you are leaving your job

The characters

Emmeline Pankhurst

1858-1928

Emmeline Pankhurst was a political activist in the UK. She is famous for campaigning for women to get the vote. She started the Women's Social and Political Union (WSPU), whose members were known as the suffragettes. Emmeline and the WSPU are famous for their militant tactics.

Christabel Harriette Pankhurst

1880-1958

Emmeline's oldest child. Christabel had a very close relationship with her mother and helped her run the WSPU. She believed the WSPU's only objective should be getting the vote for women and that only women should be allowed to join the organisation.

(Estelle) Sylvia Pankhurst

1882-1960

Emmeline's second oldest child. Sylvia worked with her mother and sister in the WSPU but she also wanted to help improve conditions for working class people, both men and women. Sylvia left the WSPU when it became more militant.

Adela Pankhurst

1885-1961

Emmeline's youngest daughter. In her early years Adela worked with her mother and sisters in the WSPU. She emigrated to Australia in 1914.

Richard Pankhurst

1834-1898

Emmeline's husband. He was a lawyer and socialist who actively supported women's rights.

Annie Kenney

1879-1953

Annie was a very active suffragette and became one of the most important people in the Women's Social and Political Union.

Herbert Henry Asquith

1852-1928

H. H. Asquith was a British politician. He was Chancellor of the Exchequer from 1905-1908 and Prime Minister from 1908-1916 for the Liberal government. Asquith did not think that women should be able to vote.

Emmeline Pethick-Lawrence

1867-1954

Emmeline Pethick-Lawrence was a socialist and a campaigner for women's rights. She organised various educational clubs and activities for working class girls, including holidays in the country. Emmeline and her husband, Frederick, started working with the WSPU in 1906 and were very important in helping the WSPU grow. Like Sylvia, they left the WSPU when it became more violent.

Chapter 1

It has been ten years since The Representation of the People
Act gave the vote to women aged 30 and over, who occupied a
house or were married to someone who did. But the same Act,
also extended the vote to every man over the age of 21, so women
still did not have the same rights as men.

However, in a few weeks' time, on 2nd July 1928, the United
Kingdom Parliament will pass a bill that will allow all women
over 21 years old to vote and women will finally be given equality.
Emmeline Pankhurst, who lies ill in a nursing home in north
London, will sadly not live to see the historic day.

Emmeline Pankhurst has been many things, a daughter, a wife,
a mother of five children, a social reformer, a widow, a suffragette,
a prisoner, a hunger striker, and a thorn in the side of the Liberal

---

21 **to extend the vote** to make the vote available to more people – 25 **equality** the same
rights for everyone in society – 26 **nursing home** a place where old people who are ill can
live and receive medical care – 29 **social reformer** sb who wants to change and improve
the way society is organised – 29 **widow** a woman whose husband is dead – 30 **hunger
striker** sb who protests about sth by refusing to eat – 30 **a thorn in the side (of sb)** sb
who causes a lot of problems for sb

government from the moment she started the Women's Social and Political Union (WSPU) in 1903 until the First World War was declared in 1914. Of all these things, suffragette, is what she is most proud of, that and her eldest daughter, Christabel. Emmeline has fought for women's suffrage for as long as she can remember, but her campaign has cost her many things, including her health and her relationships with her two other daughters, Sylvia and Adela.

As she lies in bed, too weak to read or speak to visitors, she is visited by memories from her past. She hears Christabel tell her,

"Mother, we'll get our question answered or sleep in prison tonight."

She sees her daughter holding up a Votes for Women sign and hears Annie Kenney shouting out:

"If the Liberal Party is elected, will they take steps to give votes for women?"

She sees a man put his hat over Annie's face so she can't speak and Christabel standing up to repeat the question.

"If the Liberal Party is elected, will they give women the vote?"

Emmeline had sent Christabel and Annie to a political meeting in Manchester, where the Liberal Party candidates were campaigning ahead of the next general election. It looked like the Liberal Party had enough support to be able to form the next government and take power away from the current Conservative government. Emmeline hoped that a new government would introduce legislation that would enfranchise women. Women's suffrage had been a political issue long before Emmeline Pankhurst was born in Manchester on 15th July 1858. Emmeline's parents and the man she chose to marry, Dr Richard Pankhurst, were all involved in trying to get women the right to vote in national elections, and Emmeline had started going to suffrage meeting with her mother when she was 14.

---

3 **to declare** to say sth officially and publicly – 15 **to elect** to choose a person or political party to represent you by voting for them

Emmeline wasn't at the meeting in Manchester herself, but the
story has been told to her so many times, in such detail, that it is
like the memories are her own.

Is this the beginning? Emmeline thinks. Was this the point
when I said goodbye to my previous life and became Emmeline
Pankhurst, suffragette leader and militant?

Her daughter had told her how angry the men in the crowd
were, shouting at her and Annie, telling them to shut up, and
then physically throwing them out of the meeting. For asking a
question!

Unbelievable. Men were able to ask all the questions they
wanted, but a woman speaking up at a political meeting, that
was completely different. After they had been ejected from the
meeting, Christabel and Annie were arrested by the police for
obstruction. They were given two options - pay a fine or go to jail
for one week.

Emmeline remembers hurrying to the police station to pay the
fine so she could take her daughter home. Christabel's answer
echoes in her head.

"Don't you dare, mother! If you pay the fine, I'll never come
home again. Ever!"

Emmeline smiles as she thinks how brave her daughter was
and how Christabel had stayed true to the WSPU motto, 'deeds,
not words' that day by choosing to go to prison instead of taking
the easy way out.

As more memories flood into her head, Emmeline is taken
back in time and finds herself standing at the front of a group of
around 300 women. As she looks around at the hopeful faces,

---

6 **militant** sb who believes in sth strongly and tries to cause political or social change using
force – 8 **to shut up** to stop talking – 9 **to throw sb out / to eject** to force sb to leave a
place – 15 **obstruction** stopping or delaying sth from happening – 15 **to pay a fine** to pay
money as a punishment for breaking a rule/ law – 19 **to echo** to be repeated – 20 **don't
you dare** tell sb not to do sth because you are angry about it – 23 **to stay true to sth** to
always respect and support sth even in a bad situation – 23 **motto** a short sentence that
says what an organisation believes – 23 **deed** an action sb does that is very good or very
bad – 24 **to take the easy way out** to choose the easiest option in a difficult situation

her eyes fill with tears of pride. With her, at the head of the procession, are a group of working-class women from the East End of London, friends of Sylvia's, her second oldest daughter. Behind them there are women from every other social class.

The women are all dressed in their Sunday best, most of them wearing wide-brimmed hats, some simple in style, others much more elaborate. Women with more money to spend, have hats decorated with ostrich feathers, bows, flowers and lace, one or two even have a whole bird perched on top of their heads. Appearance is very important to Emmeline Pankhurst and if the WSPU is to be seen marching through the streets of London, they must make a good impression on the people who have gathered to watch them. What is also important, is that people know who they are and what they are marching for. Sylvia is studying at the Royal College of Art and her talent for design is very useful for creating eye-catching banners, promoting the women's suffrage cause.

It is February 19th 1906, the day of the King's Speech on the opening day of Parliament, when King Edward VII will officially announce the new Liberal government's legislative plans for the year. Sylvia and Annie Kenney have organised this demonstration for the same time, hoping a show of support will encourage the government to include women's suffrage on their agenda. Sylvia has designed handbills to publicise the event, which will start with a march and then a public meeting in Caxton Hall, a 10-minute walk from the Houses of Parliament. WSPU members have worked around the clock distributing them. Chalk messages, asking

---

1 **pride** a feeling of satisfaction when you or sb connected to you has done sth good – 5 **in your Sunday best** wearing your best clothes – 6 **wide-brimmed hat** a hat with a large flat edge around the bottom – 8 **bow** a knot with two curved parts and two loose ends – 8 **lace** thin material made into a pattern with holes – 9 **to perch** to sit on the edge or top of sth – 11 **to march** to walk together in order to protest against or support sth – 11 **to make a good impression on sb** to make people think about you in a positive way – 12 **to gather** to meet together in one place and form a group – 15 **eye-catching** attractive – 16 **banner** a long piece of material with a message written on – 16 **cause** sth important a group of people support – 22 **agenda** a plan of things to be done – 23 **handbill** a small advertisement that is given to people by hand – 23 **to publicise** to tell the public about sth – 25 **to work around the clock** to work very hard all day and night – 26 **to distribute** to give sth to a lot of people

supporters to join them, have also been written on pavements all across London. Chalk is a very effective way of advertising WSPU activities. People are used to seeing children drawing pictures or the squares with numbers inside for a game of hopscotch on the pavement, but smartly dressed women on their knees writing things in chalk is something they do not see every day and it attracts more attention than a poster on a wall or a lamppost does.

As Emmeline gives the command to start walking, she can feel her heart starting to beat faster as adrenaline rushes through her body. What a great day this is going to be! She is sure that once the government hears about how dignified the marchers are and read about the clear arguments for women's suffrage that the speakers in Caxton Hall make, they will realise that women are capable of using their vote sensibly.

A large crowd has gathered to watch the march, and there are police standing along the route. The women, with their banners unfurled start to walk, but, before they can go more than a few steps, a group of policemen move towards them.

"You can't carry banners," a police inspector shouts at them. "Put them away."

"Why can't we carry banners?" Emmeline asks the inspector. "There are banners in every demonstration I've seen."

"Put them away," the inspector repeats more firmly now and nods to his colleagues, who start to move closer to the women. Mrs Pankhurst wants to have a peaceful, dignified procession so the banners are folded up and the procession for votes for women moves on to Caxton Hall for the speeches.

While Annie Kenney is on the stage speaking to the enthusiastic crowd, a messenger, who has recently arrived from

---

4 **hopscotch** a children's game where you jump between numbered squares – 7 **lamppost** a tall pole with a light on top next to a road – 9 **adrenaline** sth produced in your body when you're excited or scared that increases your energy – 9 **to rush** to move quickly – 11 **dignified** calm and serious – 17 **to unfurl** to open a banner etc that has been rolled – 23 **firmly** in a strong way – 24 **to nod** to move your head down and then up – 25 **procession** a line of people moving slowly – 29 **enthusiastic** when you show how much you like sth through your actions

Parliament, whispers to Emmeline, "The King's speech is over and there is nothing about women's suffrage." So, when Annie has finished talking and the applause has died down, Mrs Pankhurst stands up to give the bad news.

"I've just heard that the government hasn't included votes for women on their agenda. Should we wait and do nothing for another year, hoping that in the new Parliament the government will support our cause? Or should we go now, to Parliament and speak directly to the government and demand that they take action immediately?"

"To Parliament! To Parliament!" cries the audience.

The crowd of women hurries out of Caxton Hall into the cold February day. It has started raining but the bad weather is not enough to dampen their spirits and they march quickly through

---

1 **to whisper** to speak very quietly so only the person close to you can hear – 3 **applause** the noise made by a group of people clapping their hands together to show they like sth – 3 **to die down** when sth becomes much quieter – 31 **to dampen sb's spirits** to make sb's excitement less strong

the cold and rain to the public entrance to House of Commons. The policeman on guard stops them.

"Ladies, you cannot come in."

Emmeline is surprised. The doors of the House of Commons are open to all the public. This is the first time she can remember that women have not been allowed in.

"But the public galleries are open to everyone," Emmeline replies in confusion. "We have the right to enter the House!"

The policeman shakes his head. "We have our orders, Madam."

"Whose orders?"

"We have our orders," the policeman repeats. "You can't come in. Now, leave the area immediately."

Twice in one day, the police have stopped the women from doing what they have intended to do. But this time Emmeline decides they are not going to follow the police officer's orders. They had put their banners away when they were told to, after all the hard work that had gone into making them, but now this policeman is preventing them from exercising their democratic right. So, the WSPU members do not leave. They stand outside in the pouring rain and freezing cold, discussing what to do.

"Even if the new government doesn't have women's suffrage on its agenda this term, perhaps we can find a Member of Parliament who is willing to introduce a private member's bill to Parliament."

Emmeline suggests, "So, we need to find someone to tell MPs inside the House of Commons what's happening here. I'm sure many of them will be angry that we've been stopped from entering the building. If we can get a message to someone we know, I'm sure they'll be able to get us inside."

Many of the WSPU are women from the middle or upper classes of British society and they have friends, brothers, fathers or husbands in Parliament who support their cause.

---

18 **to exercise a right** to use sth you are legally allowed to do in order to make sth happen – 20 **pouring rain** very heavy rain

"Look, here's Mr Keir Hardie from the Labour Party!", says Sylvia pointing to a bearded man heading in their direction. "He supports votes for women – we should ask him to deliver our message."

Suddenly, Emmeline is aware of a bright ray of sunlight shining through the window of her room in the nursing home, warming her face. The room is clinical, all white and for a moment, she doesn't recognise where she is. "Perhaps," she thinks, "I am already dead." But then she remembers the image of a young Sylvia and the pain and anger she feels makes her realise that she is still alive. "Sylvia, what went wrong?"

Emmeline has never been as close to her middle daughter as she has to Christabel, but she still feels jealous of the very close personal and political relationship that Sylvia has developed with James Keir Hardie over the years. Then Sylvia betrayed her and the WSPU by going and living in a working-class area of London and dedicating herself to socialism. Emmeline's great cause was votes for women and she would have done, and in fact did do, anything she could do to achieve this goal, but the truth is that Mrs Emmeline Pankhurst is actually quite a conservative women. She finds Sylvia's and also Adela's support of socialist policies difficult to understand. And there is also Sylvia's pacifism. When the First World War started, Emmeline immediately ended all WSPU action and turned her energy towards supporting the war effort and encouraging men to volunteer to fight. She even urged her supporters to hand out white feathers, a symbol of cowardice,

---

2 **to head** to go towards a place – 5 **to be aware of** to realise sth is there because you can see, feel, hear, smell or feel it – 5 **ray of sunlight** a narrow line of light from the sun – 7 **clinical** without any decoration or character – 15 **to betray sb** to do sth to disappoint or hurt sb who trusts you – 17 **to dedicate yourself to sth** to give a lot of time and effort to sth you think is important – 17 **socialism** a political and social system where everyone has an equal share of the country's money – 19 **goal** objective/purpose – 20 **conservative** in favour of traditional customs and values – 22 **pacifism** belief that war and violence are wrong – 24 **the war effort** using all a country's resources to win a war – 26 **a symbol** sth used to represent another thing – 26 **cowardice** when sb who isn't brave tries to avoid danger

to any young man they found on the streets who was not wearing a military uniform.

Emmeline feels her stomach sink – 'The boy! Richard' – named after her beloved husband, dead for 30 years. And with the Pankhurst surname too – bringing disgrace on the family! She has managed to block the fact that Sylvia has had a child born out of wedlock with an Italian anarchist. The baby was born in December the previous year, but no-one had dared tell Emmeline about it because of concerns for her health. In April, when Sylvia talked about her son in an interview with a journalist, Christabel decided it was better for her mother to hear the news from a family member than read about it in a newspaper. The memory of this latest betrayal is too much for Emmeline. She tries to sit up to ring the bell on her bedside table, but she falls back onto her pillow. She really needs the nurse to come and give her something to calm her nerves.

Once a nurse has come and sedated her, Emmeline starts to drift back to that day outside the House of Commons. She hears Keir Hardie, in his strong Scottish accent, agree to take a message to other MPs. Eventually, thanks to the support of their allies inside Parliament, the policeman at the entrance reluctantly allows a small group of women to go in. But even though many MPs agree with the idea of giving women the vote, they all have other priorities, and no one is willing or able to introduce a private member's bill at the moment. So, after several hours of speaking to as many MPs as they can, the WSPU women admit defeat and leave.

---

3 **to feel your stomach sink** a physical feeling in your stomach when you start thinking about sth bad – 4 **beloved** loved very much – 5 **to bring disgrace on sb** to make people lose respect for sb because of bad behaviour – 6 **to block** to stop a memory – 7 **out of wedlock** when sb isn't married – 7 **anarchist** sb who believes laws and governments are not necessary and people should work together – 16 **to calm your nerves** to feel less angry or worried – 17 **to sedate** give sb drugs to make them sleep or calm – 18 **to drift back** to slowly start to remember – 20 **eventually** in the end – 20 **allies** people who help and support you when other people are against you – 21 **reluctantly** doing sth slowly and without enthusiasm because you don't want to do it – 24 **priorities** the most important things you need to do first – 26 **to admit defeat** to accept that you have failed

Emmeline sees herself and her children at home in the evening, sitting around the fire, drinking tea and discussing the day's events.

"Of course, I'm disappointed," Emmeline admits. "Our march wasn't the success I had hoped for. We've seen that the new government isn't interested in giving women the vote and that even the MPs who support us can't help us at the moment. On the positive side, we saw today that WSPU members are really committed to our cause - so let's not give up. Today is just the start - it's up to us women now – we're going to have to plan more direct action if we're going to persuade anyone in Parliament to introduce women's suffrage. Remember our motto! Deeds, not words will get us what we want."

"Deeds, not words!", the Pankhurst children repeat enthusiastically. They had all been united then, happier times.

Why did Emmeline Pankhurst support votes for women?

What does the WSPU motto 'Deeds, not words' mean?

Think about it...

What social, environmental or political problems are you worried about at the moment?

Would you be willing to join an organisation that campaigns for one of these causes? Why/why not?

10 **to be up to sb** be sb's responsibility – 11 **direct action** using demonstrations, strikes etc to get what you want instead of talking

Chapter 2

When Emmeline wakes up the next day, 13-year-old Mary is sitting in the chair next to her bed, with a bunch of wild flowers she has picked on Hampstead Heath. Emmeline adopted Mary and three other orphaned girls during the war. Sadly, Emmeline's financial situation and health in the last few years have been so bad that two of the children have now been adopted by other families and Christabel is taking care of another. Mary has always been Emmeline's favourite and she has done everything that she can to try to keep Mary with her, but now that Emmeline is so ill, she will need to find a new home for Mary too.

Seeing Mary helps make Emmeline feel better for a while and she is able to sit up in the bed and talk to her teenage daughter. Mary does not really know very much about her mother's past before the war and is keen to find out more before it's too late.

---

20 **Hampstead Heath** a big park in the north of London – 20 **to adopt** to take sb's child into your family and make them legally your son or daughter – 21 **orphaned** not having parents because they have died

---

"Mother, what were the suffragettes?"

Emmeline thinks back to the day she first saw that word written down. She sees herself throwing the newspaper she was reading on the floor in disgust and kicking it towards the fire...

"What is it mother?" asks Christabel.

"This man who calls himself a journalist has decided that we are not suffragists but 'suffrag-ETTES'! He wants to make fun of us, to insult us with the feminine suffix, to suggest that we are small, inferior. Hysterical little women – that's what they think we are."

Emmeline stands up, picks up the newspaper and throws it on the fire. As she watches it burst into flames and turn into ashes, she starts to smile, and turns to Christabel with a triumphant look on her face.

4 **in disgust** with a strong feeling of dislike – 7 **to make fun of sb** to laugh at sb in a cruel way – 8 **to insult** say bad things about sb – 8 **suffix** a group of letters added to the end of a word to make a different word – 9 **inferior** not as good as sth else – 9 **hysterical** crying or laughing etc without any control – 11 **to burst into flames** to start burning suddenly and strongly – 11 **ashes** the grey powder that is left after sth has been burned – 12 **triumphant** being extremely happy about a victory or success

"Let's make the word ours! Take control of it! We need to recruit a force of volunteers who will fight for votes for women and show those men what an army of suffragettes are capable of. "Later on, Emmeline is explaining her plans to Mr Keir Hardy, "… but before we can do any of this, the WSPU will need a headquarters in London where the political heart of the country is. But there is no money."

Keir Hardie proves to be a very useful friend to have.

"Let me introduce you to some people I know who I'm sure can help you. Have you heard of Mr and Mrs Pethick-Lawrence? They're very wealthy supporters of women's suffrage. As well as using their own money to support the cause, they are excellent fundraisers. She's also called Emmeline so you both have a lot in common", Keir Hardie laughs. "I'll introduce you to them both."

A few days later Emmeline visits the Pethick-Lawrences in their very large house in Clement's Inn, in central London. Mrs Pethick-Lawrence offers the WSPU the use of a room in her house while they try to raise enough money to rent an office. She imagines that the WSPU will be temporary house guests, but before too long the Pethick-Lawrence's house has become the permanent WSPU headquarters in London. After finishing her law degree, Christabel moves in with them and they end up helping her manage the business and the finances of the WSPU. Eventually, 27 of the rooms in their home will have been taken over by the WSPU.

Keir Hardie is right about the Pethick-Lawrences - they are extremely efficient organisers and fundraisers and have lots of ideas to help the WSPU grow. As well as charging a shilling to any women who wants to join the organisation, the Pethick-Lawrences decide to start an official newspaper for the WSPU,

---

2 **to recruit** persuade sb to work for an organisation – 3 **be capable of** have the ability to do sth – 6 **headquarters** the main offices of an organisation – 11 **wealthy** having a lot of money – 13 **fundraiser** sb who collects money for an organisation – 13 **to have sth in common (with sb)** to have the same characteristics, interests or ideas etc – 18 **to raise money** to collect money – 24 **to take over** to get control of – 27 **shilling** unit of money used in Britain until 1971

'Votes for Women', which they will edit. They even move a
printing press into one of their rooms so they can write, print and
distribute the paper as regularly as they want.

The first issue of 'Votes for Women' includes a photograph of
Emmeline Pankhurst, looking out from the page like a modern-
day Mona Lisa. Her wavy brown hair is swept up into a loose
bun on the top of her head, and pinned to her embroidered silk
blouse is a simple badge with the words Votes for Women. The
newspaper includes articles by Christabel and Sylvia and has a
political cartoon on the cover of each edition. It is sold on the
street, in newsagents and by subscription and in addition to
keeping readers up to date with the issue of women's suffrage, it
helps the WSPU recruit more women into the organisation, raise
money and publicise suffragette campaigns around the country.

'Votes for Women' is just one way that the suffragettes publicise
their work. They also take to the streets, taking chairs with them
until they find a good spot, where a lot of people pass by and they
are guaranteed a good crowd. Climbing onto their chairs, they
start ringing hand bells to attract attention and when enough
people have started to gather around, the suffragettes start to give
speeches about women's suffrage, answering questions from the
public and handing out pamphlets with more information. Soon,
the sound of the bell is enough for Londoners to know that the
'suffragettes' are there.

1 **to edit** to improve /correct a text – 2 **printing press** machine used for printing
newspapers,books etc – 6 **Mona Lisa** a famous painting of a woman smiling by Leonardo
Da Vinci – 6 **wavy (hair)** in between straight and curly – 6 **to sweep up hair into
loose bun** to twist long hair into a round shape and lift it to the top or back of sb's
head – 7 **embroidered** decorated cloth with designs stitched into it with coloured
thread – 8 **badge** a small piece of flat metal or plastic with words or a picture on that you
can fasten to your clothes – 10 **edition** a newspaper or magazine in a regular series –
11 **newsagent's** a shop that sells newspapers and magazines etc – 11 **by subscription**
paying money in advance to receive a newspaper or magazine regularly – 16 **to take to the
streets** to go out to the streets to protest – 18 **to guarantee** to be certain sth will happen
– 22 **pamphlet** a thin book with only a few pages

Mary cannot imagine the mother she knows standing on a chair in the middle of the street, ringing a bell.

"I did that and more," Emmeline tells her. "I went around the country wherever there were by-elections heckling politicians!"

Mary cannot believe her ears. This small, frail woman, who is so proper in her behaviour, insulting people in public.

"There was one politician in particular…," Emmeline pauses as she thinks about Herbert Henry Asquith, "who did everything he could to stop women getting the vote. The Prime Minister, Sir Henry Campbell-Bannerman was sympathetic to our cause, but he told us we had to be patient because women's suffrage didn't have the support of the government. Our main opponent was Asquith, the Chancellor of the Exchequer."

"So what did you do?"

---

21 **to heckle** to interrupt a speech by shouting questions or insults – 22 **to not believe your ears** to be very surprised about sth you hear – 22 **frail** not very strong or healthy – 27 **to be sympathetic to sth** to support sth – 29 **opponent** sb who is against sth and tries to stop it

Emmeline, Christabel and Annie Kenney are planning what
action to take now that Prime Minister has confirmed the Liberal
government will not be enfranchising women in the near future.
"We must make our voices louder," Christabel says.
"I agree," Emmeline replies. "Asking polite questions and
petitioning Parliament and the Prime Minister hasn't got us
anywhere."
"We should follow the lead of the men themselves," adds Annie.
"The opposition parties in the House of Commons are always
interrupting the government and not with polite questions either.
They shout insults at them and try to stop them debating any bill
they don't agree with. Then you read the newspaper reports where
the journalists say how clever the insults are, and what a good job
they've done not allowing their opponents to speak!"
"Then we'll do the same!" Emmeline says as she starts to put a
plan together in her head.
Members of the WSPU start to disrupt political meetings up
and down the country, not only by asking questions about votes
for women, but by heckling the members of the government
whenever they try to speak. As Asquith is one of the biggest
anti-suffragette politicians in the Liberal government, Emmeline
decides they need to take the campaign to his door. She is in the
north of England campaigning against the Liberal candidate in a
local by-election, so she sends a group of women to visit Asquith
in his home. The idea is to try and speak directly to him and ask
him why he is against giving women the vote. When they get to
his house, once again they are stopped from achieving their goal
by the police. A struggle breaks out between the police and the
suffragettes, as the women try to reach Asquith's door. Asquith,

---

3 **the near future** soon – 6 **to petition** to formally ask for sth – 6 **to not get anywhere**
to not make progress – 8 **to follow the lead (of sb)** to do the same thing sb else has
done – 11 **to debate** to discuss sth formally before making a decision – 15 **to put a plan
together** to prepare a plan by organising ideas – 17 **to disrupt** to make it difficult for sth
to continue normally – 28 **struggle** a physical fight – 28 **to break out** to start suddenly

who is watching from inside, starts to feel nervous, as the women become more determined to reach his house. One of them breaks free from the police and makes a run for the door so Asquith decides that the best option is to leave. He escapes through his back door and is driven away to safety. One WSPU member manages to force her way inside Asquith's home and another climbs on top of his car to make a political speech, which she hopes the Chancellor will hear, but since Asquith has gone, all that happens is that the police arrest her and some of the other suffragettes for causing a disturbance.

Just as the suffragettes have increased their forces and improved their organisation, so too have the police. In February 1907, with Emmeline still in the north, Christabel leads a march of suffragettes to the House of Commons in protest against another King's Speech which does not include any reference to women's suffrage. There are many more policemen than before guarding the entrance to Parliament and to strengthen their defences they have added a group of mounted police. The women of the WSPU try hard to get in, but against police on horses, it is an almost impossible task. Nearly 60 people are arrested and sent to prison including Christabel and Sylvia.

Mary is surprised that her Aunt Christabel, who she knows as a very religious women was sent to jail when she was younger.

"Did you ever go to prison?" she asks Emmeline nervously, but before her mother can tell her anything else, a nurse comes into the room to tell Mary that Emmeline needs to rest, and it is time for her to go.

As Mary is taken out of the room, she looks back one more time at her mother. As she does, a cloud covers the sun for a moment, and a shadow passes over Emmeline, who is now lying

---

2 **determined** not allowing anyone to stop you from doing what you have decided to do – 2 **to break free** to escape – 3 **to make a run for ...** to start running somewhere in order to escape – 10 **disturbance** a situation where people behave violently – 17 **to strengthen** to make stronger – 18 **mounted police** police riding horses – 20 **an almost impossible task** sth that is very difficult to do

down on the bed with her eyes closed. Mary starts to cry. She has a horrible feeling that she will not see her mother again.

How did the Pethick-Lawrences help the WSPU?

How did the WSPU publicise their work?

Think about it...

The WSPU could not use social media. How does social media and the internet help organisations to publicise their campaigns?

Is there anything you have discovered about somebody in your family that has surprised you?

Chapter 3

Did you ever go to prison? Oh yes… thinks Emmeline as she slips into a restless sleep.

"Will these women never stop?" the Crown Prosecutor Mr Muskett asks the Home Secretary Herbert Gladstone, when he has yet another a group of suffragettes in court for disorderly conduct. "They've ignored every warning they've been given and now it's like they're queuing up to go to prison. It's like Holloway is the French Riviera, the number of them wanting to go there."

Gladstone agrees, "I've never seen anything like it. So-called respectable women fighting the police. The younger generation are more badly behaved than before but some of these women are our age or even older. If we're not careful this trouble will spread

---

19 **to slip into a restless sleep** to slowly fall asleep but keep waking up often – 20 **the Crown Prosecutor** an official who is responsible for proving in a law court that sb is guilty of a crime – 22 **disorderly conduct** behaving badly – 24 **Holloway** a prison for women in London – 25 **the French Riviera** an attractive part of the Mediterranean coast in France – 26 **so-called** used to show you think a word that is used to describe sb or sth is not correct – 29 **to spread to** to affect more people, places or things

to the lower classes and then we'll be in trouble. If only we could arrest them just for standing outside of Parliament with a sign."

"Hmm, I think I might have just the thing," Mr Muskett says thoughtfully. "The Tumultuous Petitions Act. It was a law under King Charles II that made it illegal for anyone to take a petition or complaint to Parliament if they had more than 10 other people with them. It's a £100 fine or three months in prison."

"Really?" Mr Gladstone asks in surprise. He had not actually been serious about arresting people just for being together in group. But now, thinking about it, perhaps this law could be useful. "Perhaps, we don't have to actually use the law. We can just spread a rumour that we're planning to use it.

When that Pankhurst woman hears about it, I'm sure she'll think twice about marching on Parliament with all her supporters."

But the opposite is true. Emmeline is keen to see if the government is bluffing or not. Another year has passed with no mention of women's suffrage in the King's Speech and it is now February 1908.

"Who is prepared to join me and take a petition to the House of Commons?" Emmeline tells WSPU's members at the end of their meeting. "I only need eleven women to come with me to challenge the government. But those eleven need to be prepared to be arrested. I am, are you?"

A large number of hands go up in the crowd of women.

"If they want to arrest twelve women, here are those twelve. And when us twelve are arrested, here are twelve more. If the government wants to arrest a hundred women, they can be found here in this hall right now!"

Emmeline and the eleven volunteers leave to go to Parliament.

---

3 **just the thing** exactly what you need – 4 **thoughtfully** in way that shows you are thinking a lot about sth – 5 **King Charles II** King of England from 1630 to 1685 – 5 **illegal** now allowed by law – 9 **to be serious** to not joke about sth – 12 **rumour** a story that may not be true that everyone is talking about – 13 **to think twice about sth** to think very carefully before deciding to do sth – 16 **to bluff** to try to make sb believe that you will do sth when you do not intend to

"Are you alright Emmeline?" asks Flora Drummond, one the WSPU inner circle. "You're limping. Is this from when you were attacked by that group of ruffians in the Midlands?" Emmeline had been campaigning at a by-election when things turned nasty. A group of young men had attacked her and knocked her to the ground. She had been lucky to escape with only a twisted ankle. A shopkeeper had rescued her and locked her inside the shop until the police arrived.

"You're obviously in pain. I don't think you should walk any further. Look! Here's a man with a cart. I'll stop him and ask him to drive you to the House of Commons."

Emmeline is helped onto the cart and her eleven companions walk in line behind. But they have not gone very far when they find a large group of policemen waiting for them on the road.

2 **to limp** to walk with difficulty because your leg or foot is hurt – 3 **ruffian** a violent man – 4 **to turn nasty** to become violent – 6 **twisted ankle** an injury when you turn your ankle in bad way – 7 **shopkeeper** sb who owns a small shop – 10 **cart** an old-fashioned wooden vehicle used for carrying things

"Stop where you are. That cart can't go any further," one of the policemen commands, looking at the line of women. It appears he is counting how many of them there are. "You can get off the cart and walk in single file."

Flora Drummond tries to explain to the policeman that Emmeline cannot walk without help but he is not listening to her. So Emmeline is forced to limp along on her own. She manages to go a short distance but in addition to the group of police, a large crowd has gathered and it is difficult for the women to push their way through. The pain from her ankle is so bad now that Emmeline thinks she is going to faint.

"Flora, can you and Annie help me? I don't think I can go on any further without support". Emmeline puts her arms around her two companions who have moved to either side of her.

All of a sudden, two burly policemen grab her.

"You're all under arrest. You were told to walk in single file and you've blatantly disobeyed police orders." Emmeline is carried away to a police car.

In court the next day, the suffragettes are shocked to hear the prosecutor tell the judge, "My Lord these women are here today for disorderly conduct. They were shouting and singing and behaving very badly for women. When the police officers asked them to behave in a more ladylike way, they responded with insults and physical violence and started knocking policemen's helmets off their heads."

"These are lies!" Emmeline cries, standing up to speak in her defence. "There are witnesses here in this courtroom who can tell you that we were walking peacefully and did nothing wrong."

---

2 **to command** when a person in a position of authority tells sb to do sth – 4 **in single file** walking one person behind the other – 11 **to faint** to become unconscious – 15 **burly** a large and strong person – 17 **blatantly** in an obvious and intentional way – 18 **to disobey** to refuse to do what sb tells you to – 23 **ladylike** polite and quiet – 27 **witness** sb who sees sth happen eg an accident or crime – 27 **courtroom** the room where a legal court meets

"Madam, you will sit down and stay silent," she is told by the judge. "You are sentenced to six weeks in prison."

Emmeline and the other suffragettes are taken to Holloway women's prison in north London, where Sylvia and Christabel have both served their sentences.

"Take off your clothes," a wardress orders Mrs Pankhurst. Mrs Pankhurst takes off her dress and then stops.

"Take off everything!"

Instead of her beautiful, elegant clothes, she is handed a pile of prison clothes to put on. Her daughters have told her what to expect in prison, but for a 50-year-old woman, so careful about her appearance, she cannot help but be disgusted at what she is expected to wear. She does not want to think about how many times the dirty, old underwear has been worn or when it was last washed.

Then there are brown woollen stockings with red stripes, which will make her legs itch, along with a shapeless dark dress stamped with thick white arrows so everyone knows she is a prisoner. Finally, to complete the outfit, there is an apron with black arrows printed on, to wear over the dress.

"Follow me now to your cell."

As the door slams shut behind her, Emmeline looks around the small, dark and damp cell where she is expected to spend the first month of her prison sentence in solitary confinement. The smell makes her nauseous, and there is no fresh air to help clear her head. At night, the cell is freezing and the sheets she has

---

2 **to be sentenced** to be told in court what punishment you will get for a crime –
6 **wardress** a female officer in charge of prisoners in a jail – 9 **elegant** good sense of style – 16 **woollen** made of wool - the hair of a sheep – 16 **stockings** clothes for the feet and legs usually worn under skirts or dresses – 17 **to itch** to cause an uncomfortable feeling on your skin so you want to rub it with your nails – 17 **shapeless** not having a defined form – 17 **stamped** printed – 18 **arrow** a sign in the form of a straight line with a V shape on its side at its end used to show direction – 19 **outfit** a group of clothes you wear together – 19 **apron** sth you wear over your normal clothes to protect them eg when you are cooking – 21 **cell** a room for a prisoner – 22 **to slam** to shut noisily with force – 23 **damp** slightly wet – 24 **solitary confinement** a punishment where sb is kept in a room alone – 25 **nauseous** feeling like you want to vomit

been given are not enough to keep her warm. Although she is exhausted, Emmeline cannot sleep on the hard prison bed, and spends her first night shivering in the cold. In the morning, she feels very ill. During solitary confinement, there is no contact with other prisoners or access to books or pens and papers so she must sit alone, with nothing to do except think. There is an hour of silent exercise in a cold courtyard, which is the only thing that breaks up the day.

After two days, the wardress sees that she needs medical treatment, and she is sent to the hospital. The bed in the hospital is slightly more comfortable and Emmeline is finally able to sleep. But in the middle of the night, she is woken up by the noise of a woman groaning loudly. A baby is being born in another cell. Emmeline is horrified to think that a child is starting life in such a terrible place and cannot go back to sleep that night. After the first month is over, she is given a slate to write on and a book to read and with these two simple things she passes the time until she is released.

What was the Tumultuous Petitions Act?

What were the conditions like in Holloway prison?

---

3 **to shiver** when your body shakes because you are cold or frightened – 7 **courtyard** an open area surrounded by buildings or walls – 13 **to groan** to make a long deep sound because you are in pain – 14 **horrified** very shocked or frightened – 16 **slate** a flat piece of grey stone used in the past for writing on with chalk

Think about it...

What are the laws about protesting in your country. Do you think you could be arrested for only holding a sign?

If you were in solitary confinement without access to anything, how could you pass the time?

Chapter 4

The day after Mary's visit Emmeline is feeling worse and cannot think straight. To try and focus her mind, she tries to replay the conversation she had with her adopted daughter. She knows they talked about Asquith. How could she ever forget that man?

'I may not have much longer left,' she thinks, 'but at least I have the satisfaction of knowing that in the end I have outlived my old rival, despite all the suffering he has caused me.'

Asquith becomes Prime Minister on 5th April 1908 and almost immediately announces his plans to introduce a reform bill which will give the vote to a wider group of men. For Emmeline, it is like a slap in the face. However, some of the Liberal party supporters believe that Asquith will allow a women's suffrage amendment to be added to the bill as long as it has the support of the electorate and the majority of women of the country. Emmeline tells everyone they are being fooled by the Prime Minister and that he does not have any intention of supporting an amendment.

Emmeline and Christabel are discussing what will happen now that Asquith is in charge of the Liberal government. They are both very interested in a recent speech given by the Home Secretary, Herbert Gladstone.

"So even though Mr Gladstone has been trying to find ways to stop the suffragettes protesting by locking us up in prison whenever he can, he's now announced that he will, in fact, vote in favour of a women's suffrage bill. Listen to this," Emmeline starts to read out Mr Gladstone's speech which has been printed in the newspaper. "Men know that to show they have support for reforms they must gather in tens of thousands all over the country, he says. Power belongs to the masses and this power

---

2 **cannot think straight** cannot think clearly and calmly – 3 **to replay** to think about something again and again – 7 **to outlive** to live longer than sb – 8 **rival** sb you are competing or fighting against – 8 **suffering** the physical or mental pain that sb is feeling – 12 **slap** when you hit sb with the flat part of your hand – 16 **to be fooled by** to believe sth that sb tells you when it's not true – 30 **the masses** the ordinary people in society

can influence a government. The suffragist women only have the support of a few hundred people – only enough to fill a public hall. They do not have the support of thousands and without these number they are unable to influence anyone."

"So," says Christabel, "he doesn't think that a bill will pass because there isn't enough political or public support."

"But is he suggesting that if we gather together tens of thousands of supporters, the government will be forced to act? Here in the paper, they say that when men were trying to get a vote, the largest crowd of demonstrators in Hyde Park was 72,000. Well! I believe that we can get at least three times that number. What do you think, Christabel? 250,000 people in Hyde Park demanding votes for women - can we do that?"

"Now we're organised and we have the Pethick-Lawrence's on our side, anything is possible!"

Women's Sunday, the biggest demonstration that London has seen will be held on June 21st 1908. Details have been published in 'Votes for Women' over several editions. WSPU members are told to spend the days before the 21st advertising the seven processions which will march to Hyde Park.

Handbills are distributed outside underground stations and on buses, trams and trains as well as at schools, hospitals, and clubs. WSPU members talk to London shop assistants, waitresses and other females workers and invite them to join the processions. Posters are put up in shop windows and announcements are chalked on pavements calling all the public, men and women, to join the demonstration.

The processions have been organised with military efficiency by Mrs Pethick-Lawrence. Flora Drummond will be the 'General' in control of all the processions. Then there will be a series of marshals responsible for each of the seven processions and each

10 **Hyde Park** a large park in the centre of London – 14 **on your side** supporting you – 31 **marshal** an official who supervises a public event

procession will be divided up into sections with group captains in charge. People are expected from over 70 towns from around the country and Mrs Pethick-Lawrence has organised WSPU officials to meet the demonstrators from the trains, some that have been especially booked and paid for by the WSPU.

In Hyde Park, there will be recruiting sergeants, WSPU members wearing purple, green and white rosettes, who will show people where to go and take the names and addresses of people who want to join the WSPU.

"Mrs Pethick-Lawrence, I cannot tell you how pleased I am with the WSPU colours you have come up with!" Emmeline tells her colleague a few days before the great event. "White for purity, purple for loyalty and dignity and green for hope. They represent

6 **sergeant** an officer in the army or police – 29 **to come up with** to think of an idea – 30 **purity** clean or morally good – 31 **loyalty** complete support for sth – 31 **dignity** a calm and serious manner

everything we stand for. Sylvia's working on some new jewellery designs that incorporate the colours to go with the badges and pins we already have. She even has an idea for a design for tea sets. Who knows, perhaps one day, every woman in the country will be pouring their husband's tea from a suffragette teapot into a suffragette teacup!"

Mrs Pethick-Lawrence laughs at the idea. "We'll see. As you know we're asking all the women to wear a white or cream dress on Sunday and if we can get them to add a purple, white and green WSPU scarf, ribbon or sash as well, it will be quite the spectacle. We want our colours to be so well known that every fashionable woman in Britain will want to wear them. When our colours are instantly recognised, then we won't even need slogans. Even someone who doesn't know how to read will instantly know that purple, white and green mean votes for women."

"Quite the opposite of how the suffragettes are portrayed in newspaper cartoons. They always draw suffragettes as a woman so plain and masculine that no man would want to marry her. I saw one yesterday where the woman had a moustache so thick, she looked like Herbert Gladstone. Absolutely ridiculous! That's why it's so important that we always look our feminine best so there's no truth at all in those cartoons. We are not spinsters – angry because we can't find a husband – no, we are wives and mothers angry about our oppression!"

A journalist for The Times estimates that if the WSPU had counted on 250,000 people attending Women's Sunday, the reality was that there were double that number, or even possibly treble. In 'Votes for Women' Mrs Pethick-Lawrence is confident enough

1 **to stand for** to represent a particular idea – 3 **tea set** a small set of matching plates, cups etc for serving tea – 10 **ribbon** a long narrow piece of cloth eg for tying hair – 10 **sash** a long piece of cloth worn over one shoulder or around your waist with formal or official clothes – 11 **spectacle** an event that is exciting to look at – 13 **slogan** a short sentence used to advertise an idea or product – 22 **spinster** a woman who has never been married – 24 **oppression** when people are governed in an unfair way and are not given the same rights as others

to say that it was the largest ever number of people gathered together in one place, at one time, in the history of the world.

If half a million men and women from all over England had turned up to show their support for women's suffrage, surely that would be more than enough to influence Mr Herbert Henry Asquith and his Liberal government?

'But,' thinks Emmeline feeling the same frustration she had felt all those years ago, 'it wasn't enough, was it?'

Why did the WSPU organise Women's Sunday?

Why were the colours white, purple and green important for the WSPU?

Think about it... ◆

Have there been any big demonstrations where you live recently? What for and were they successful?

What colours would you choose to represent yourself?

---

4 **to turn up** to arrive

Chapter 5

"I refuse to speak to that woman!" Asquith mutters, handing a letter from Mrs Pankhurst back to the police inspector who has brought it to him. "When she and her suffragettes come to the Parliament at half-past four, make sure she is not allowed to enter. "

"Is there any message that you want me to give her, sir?"

"There is no message. Give the letter back to her. Do not let her inside." "Very well, sir."

The Home Secretary, who is sitting in a corner, sighs. "Asquith, why are you against giving women the vote? There is public support – you read the reports in the papers about the turnout for the march to Hyde Park. 500,000 people attended, they say. All peaceful and respectable. Why, my wife even went along to see what it was all about. She was impressed by how well it was organised and thought Mrs Pankhurst spoke well."

"The Pankhursts are an annoying distraction. The government has more important things to do than worry about silly women wanting to play at politics. How does she think that I would give women the vote before all the men in the country have been enfranchised? Besides, what do women know about how a country is run? Most are completely uninformed about politics and the wider world. We cannot trust them to make the right decisions about the defence of the British Empire."

"But the way that these women's suffrage organisations are run is very impressive. They are organised almost like an army! And they are effective political machines too. Look at how they've influenced the number of votes for Liberal candidates in by-elections up and down the country with their campaigning – some of our candidates have lost a lot of votes because of them."

---

1 **to mutter** to say sth in a quiet voice so it is not easy to hear especially when you are angry about sth – 9 **to sigh** to breathe out slowly and noisily to show you are tired, sad or disappointed – 11 **turnout** the number of people who attend an event – 16 **distraction** sth that stops sb from giving their attention to sth else – 21 **uninformed** having no information or knowledge about sth

"Shouting down politicians when they're trying to speak is not political campaigning!" Asquith replies angrily. "What? Why do you find that funny, Gladstone?"

"Isn't that exactly what we did to the Conservatives when they were in power?" Asquith scowls at the Home Secretary. He is not in the mood for this conversation.

"Gladstone, women have their sphere of political influence in local affairs. They are on the boards that run housing, education, the care of children and workhouses. National affairs do NOT concern them – they have their husbands and fathers to represent them there. Anyway, as you know, most women are naturally conservative so if we did enfranchise them, they would vote us out of government at the next election and the Conservative Party would be back in power for a very long time."

The last point, Gladstone agrees with.

Later in the evening Gladstone is at the entrance to the House of Commons with the same police inspector who delivered Mrs Pankhurst's letter to Asquith. Neither man is very happy. Thousands of people are in Parliament Square, not only the suffragettes and their supporters but also groups of rowdy young men who have come to cause trouble. For several hours, the mounted police try to move the crowd away from Parliament Square, and it is not until midnight that they succeed.

'This is the point that marked the beginning of a new kind of militant campaign,' Emmeline thinks. 'When the suffragettes became famous, or rather infamous, throughout the country. Who was it again? Ah, yes, Mrs Mary Leigh and Miss Edith New. They were the ones who threw stones through Asquith's window at 10 Downing Street.' She laughs to herself as she imagines Asquith's face.

---

1 **to shout sb down** to stop sb from speaking by shouting at them – 5 **to scowl** to look at sb in an angry or annoyed way – 7 **sphere of influence** an area where sb has the power to control sth – 20 **rowdy** making a lot of noise or causing trouble – 24 **to mark sth** to be a sign that something new is going to happen – 26 **infamous** famous for sth bad

Then less happy memories come as Emmeline remembers herself in Holloway again, not as a prisoner but to visit the stone-throwing suffragettes.

"We understand if you don't want to support us Emmeline," Mrs Leigh says. "We acted unofficially and don't want the WSPU to take the blame."

"Don't worry Mary, I completely approve of your actions. Window-breaking has always been a legitimate way for the public to show that they're against the government's policies. Remember the Duke of Wellington had to have iron shutters added to all his windows to protect him from the anger of his opponents. I'm proud of you both but sorry that the government sees your protest as a common crime and not an act of political protest."

Every time they have been arrested and sent to Holloway, the suffragettes ask to be treated as political prisoners and not common criminals. Political prisoners are put in a different section of the prison, the first division, where they can order their own food, wear their own clothes and have more comforts. But, every time the prison authorities refuse and put them in the second or third division where the conditions are much, much worse.

"I don't see we have any choice now Emmeline. If the government oppresses us, we have to resort to stronger action. This fight is going to continue."

'So many women were willing to give up their freedom for our cause,' thinks Emmeline proudly. And her thoughts turn to Marion Wallace Dunlop, another Suffragette to go to Holloway.

Marion Wallace Dunlop is arrested for printing an extract from the 1689 Bill of Rights, which established basic civil rights in England, onto the wall of the House of Commons in ink, which is

---

6 **to take the blame** to say that you did sth – 10 **the Duke of Wellington** British Prime Minister 1834 and 1828-1830 – 10 **shutters** covers on the outside of a window made of wood or metal – 23 **to resort to** to do sth because there is no other way to achieve sth – 28 **extract** a specific part of a written text

certainly more difficult to remove than chalk and so she is sent to Holloway.

Just like Mary Leigh and Edith New, Marion Wallace Dunlop decides to take her own militant action without the WSPU's permission. Marion says that she is going on hunger strike and will not eat anything until the government agrees to recognise her as a political prisoner and move her to the first division.

After a week of hunger strike, she is released from prison and sent home. Once they hear of her release, other WSPU prisoners immediately decide to follow her example. They refuse to eat, to put on the prison uniform and to keep the rule of silence. They are all released before the week is over.

'We caught the government by surprise, didn't we?', thinks Emmeline. 'No one would ever have imagined that women would take such drastic action, that they believed in their cause so

30 **to catch sb by surprise** to surprise sb when they are not expecting it – 32 **drastic** sth extreme

strongly that they would willingly starve themselves to death and make themselves martyrs.'

But as more of the WSPU prisoners start to refuse food, the government decides to take drastic steps of their own.

The WSPU committee are listening in horrified silence to the account of Mrs Leigh, who has been on hunger strike in Birmingham jail.

"Two doctors took me to a room with a big wooden chair in the middle of it. There were four wardresses standing against the wall and one of the doctor's told me that if I didn't eat, they'd make me. I knew that I couldn't be legally force fed without giving my permission because they can only do that if a patient is certified insane. But then I saw the rubber tube - it must have been about two yards long and that's when I started to get scared. Then the wardresses pushed me onto the chair and held me down. The doctor started to force the tube up my nose. I've never felt so much pain, I was screaming for them to stop but the doctor just kept pushing it up my nose and down my throat and then I couldn't scream any more. They poured liquid into the tube through a funnel and I couldn't breathe. I thought I was going to die then. I told myself it couldn't get any worse, but it did. When they pulled the tube out, it was like my nose and throat were being pulled out too. The pain was horrific."

As much as Emmeline dislikes Asquith, she cannot believe that the government would use such shocking tactics against anyone.

"They are force feeding our women! Forcing tubes down their throats and calling it 'Hospital treatment'!"

---

1 **to starve** to become very weak or die because you do not have enough food to eat – 2 **martyr** sb who is killed or suffers because of their beliefs – 11 **to be force fed** to be made to eat and drink by force – 13 **to be certified insane** a legal document that states sb is mentally ill – 14 **yard** a unit for measuring length in the UK and USA (2 yards = 1.8 m) – 15 **to hold sb down** to stop sb from moving using force – 20 **funnel** an object with a wide circular top and a narrow bottom used to pour liquids into bottles – 23 **horrific** extremely bad and frightening – 25 **tactics** plans used to achieve sth

Why did Asquith not want to give the vote to women?

Why did Marion Wallace Dunlop go on hunger strike?

Think about it...

Do you think it was an easy decision for the Government to make when they decided to force feed the prisoners? Why/why not?

If you were asked by somebody in authority to do something that you thought was wrong, what would you do?

Chapter 6

Emmeline still finds it difficult to remind herself that even though shocking stories of women being force fed were in all the national newspapers, the Liberal Party were still voted into power again in 1910. Asquith, her arch-enemy, was still Prime Minister but without as big as majority as before and he had to rely on the Labour Party MPs to govern.

'With more supporters in the House of Commons, I really believed that women's suffrage could finally be achieved,' she remembers. 'We even had a bill introduced to Parliament that would have given the vote to women householders and enough votes for the bill to reach a final reading. But no, Asquith decided there was not enough time for the Conciliation Bill to go any further in the current parliament. I should have known!'

'And then came Black Friday...'

"Asquith is a monster," Emmeline declares to her daughters as they relive the events of Friday 18th November. "He has betrayed us time and time again. He has treated us worse than murderers in prison, force feeding us and now this! Using police violence on us as we peacefully protest against his refusal to allow the Conciliation Bill to become law."

"I have never seen an assault like this before," Sylvia adds. "I saw women being treated indecently at the hands of plain clothes police. Many of our members were humiliated. The police officers were beating women all over their bodies, throwing women from one man to another. I saw a women crushed under the hooves of a police horse after an officer threw her onto the ground!"

"Yet our women kept on trying to reach the House of Commons to get their voices heard despite their cuts and bruises," Emmeline replies.

---

4 **arch-enemy** most important enemy – 5 **majority** the number of votes a political party wins an election by – 6 **to govern** to control and direct a country, city etc – 10 **householder** sb who owns or rents the house/flat they live in – 21 **assault** a physical attack – 22 **indecently** in a way that is morally offensive – 22 **plain clothes police** police who are not wearing a uniform – 23 **humiliated** make sb feel ashamed or stupid – 24 **to beat** to hit sb very hard – 25 **to be crushed** to be pressed very hard – 25 **hooves** the hard part of an animal like a horse or cow's feet – 28 **bruise** dark mark on your skin when you have been hit by sth

"And did you hear that May Billinghurst was assaulted? A women in a wheelchair! They took her down a side street and threw her out of her chair and then left her in the middle of a crowd of rowdy hooligans. And, before they left her, they took the valves out of the tyres on her chair so she had no way of escaping. What kind of men do that?" asks Christabel angrily.

"They're trying to frighten us now with physical violence. Showing us that we can't stop them physically because they're stronger than us and if they want to, they can really hurt us. It's true that individually we may be weaker than them, but together as an army, we'll show them how strong we can be! If they think they can scare us into going back to our homes and staying there, then they're wrong!" Emmeline replies.

'And so another year went by,' Emmeline recalls, 'and more disappointments, but we answered back with militancy of our own. The only thing that Asquith seemed to understand.'

In 1911, Asquith announces that the Liberals will introduce a new bill to give more men the right to vote with no mention of votes for women. For the sixth time since Asquith has become Prime Minister, Emmeline and the WSPU write to him to ask him to meet a deputation from the Union. To their surprise, this time Asquith agrees to meet them and deputations from other suffrage societies.

The Prime Minister tells the women that he has done what he promised and allowed MPs to introduce bills for women's suffrage, but that his priority is to give more men the vote.

On Tuesday 21st November, several days after the unsuccessful meeting with Mr Asquith, hundreds of WSPU supporters dressed in long coats and veiled hats, calmly take to the streets and at precisely 8pm, start breaking the windows of government offices

---

4 **hooligan** sb behaving in a noisy and violent way in public – 5 **valve** a device that allows air to be added or removed – 15 **militancy** using force to cause political or social change – 21 **deputation** a group of people speaking or acting for others – 29 **veiled hat** a hat with a thin piece of material attached that covers the face

on Whitehall with the stones and hammers they have hidden
in their pockets or bags. At the end of the evening nearly every
window in the area, except for Downing Street, which is heavily
guarded, has a large round hole in the middle. The suffragettes
have started a new level of militant action. Window breaking
expands to arson as Emily Wilding Davison is sent to prison for
six months in December 1911, for setting fire to a letter box at
Parliament Street Post Office.

'Oh, poor Emily,' Emmeline feels her eyes fill with tears as she
thinks about what happened to Emily in the end. But she has not
got to that point yet, and pushes the memory of that particular
tragedy to the back of her mind.

1 **hammer** a tool used for hitting things – 6 **arson** the crime of setting fire to sth on
purpose – 7 **to set fire to** to make sth start to burn – 7 **letter box** an opening in a door or
wall where mail is delivered – 29 **to push sth to the back of your mind** to try not to think
about sth – 3 **tragedy** an extremely sad event

"We've reached a point where we can see that having the
sympathy of some members of Parliament is no use to our cause."
Emmeline announces as she addresses a meeting of the WSPU
in 1912. "We must prepare ourselves for more action. We're
here to welcome back our members who've been released from
prison after November's window-breaking campaign. I really
believe that the argument of the broken pane of glass is the most
valuable argument in modern politics. Every advance in men's
political freedom has involved the destruction of property. If this
weapon is sufficient, then we will never have to use any stronger
argument. So, I call on every volunteer here – be prepared to
use that argument! It's the one that the government appears to
understand. We've seen that when we take petitions peacefully to
Parliament, we're assaulted and hurt. Isn't a woman's safety more
valuable than a pane of glass?"

Mrs Pankhurst speech is reported back to the government,
and she is accused of inciting violence and destruction of
property. The WSPU has announced a demonstration on March
4th using their normal methods of publicity and so the police
and government start making plans to stop the suffragette
protest. What they do not know is that the WSPU has planned
another secret demonstration on the 1st. Emmeline and three
companions take a taxi to No. 10 Downing Street, they get out
and before they can be stopped, each woman throws a stone
through the Prime Minister's window. This is the first action in
an hour-long campaign of smashing shop windows along the
fashionable shopping streets of London. Every 15 minutes, the
sound of breaking glass rings out as a small group of women
walk down a street, calmly breaking the glass in the windows of
shop after shop after shop, until no window is left intact. While

---

3 **to address** to speak to – 7 **pane** a flat sheet of glass in a window or door – 17 **to incite**
to encourage sb to do sth violent or illegal – 26 **to smash** to break into many pieces –
28 **to ring out** to be heard loudly and clearly – 30 **intact** complete and not broken

the police run to arrest them, another group starts breaking the
windows in a street further away.

Mrs Pankhurst and a large number of other women are taken
to police stations and the police hurry to the WSPU headquarters
to arrest Christabel and Mr and Mrs Pethick-Lawrence on the
charge of conspiring to incite WSPU members to commit damage
to property. Christabel is luckier than the Pethick-Lawrences
and manages to escape. In Clements Inn, police officers fill boxes
full of WSPU record books and papers as evidence against the
organisation. They search railways stations and ports trying to
find Christabel, but they are too late - Christabel has already
made her way safely across the English Channel, where she is
travelling to Paris.

During the trial, the suffragettes learn that there is a special
group of secret police in England who are employed for political
purposes. Seventy-five undercover police officers have been
following the suffragettes and other political groups from their
homes to their work, to tea rooms where they meet their friends,
to the theatres where they go for their entertainment. They
follow people in taxis and sit beside them on the bus without
their suspects ever knowing. One of their main jobs is to go to
meetings and write down the speeches that are made there, word
for word. It is thanks to these secret police that the government
knows about Mrs Pankhurst's speech inciting violence and the
destruction of property.

Emmeline is allowed to make a passionate speech in her
defence, outlining the history of the WSPU, explaining why they
have been forced to resort to window breaking and insisting that
their actions are political. Despite the power of her argument,

5 **on the charge of** the crime the police say you have committed – 6 **to conspire** to make
a secret agreement with other people to do sth illegal – 12 **the English** – 12 **Channel**
the sea between England and France – 16 **undercover police** police working secretly in
order to find out information – 22 **word for word** repeated exactly as said or written –
26 **passionate** with very strong feelings or emotions

Emmeline and the Pethick-Lawrences are sentenced to nine months in prison as common criminals.

Why was Friday 18ᵗʰ November known as Black Friday?

Why did Emmeline Pankhurst support window breaking?

Think about it...

Do you think political crimes are different to 'common' crimes?

If this was today, do you think Christabel would be able to escape to another country and continue organising the campaign? Why/why not?

Chapter 7

"They say when you die, your life flashes before you",
Emmeline says weakly to Christabel who has come to visit. "I've
been reliving all the things that happened before the war over the
last few days. If what they say is true, then my death is happening
very slowly."

Christabel looks at her mother lying there. She looks so small
and frail that Christabel believes she could lift her up using only
one hand. A once strong, fierce fighter, reduced to a shadow of
her former self, exhausted by her determination to achieve her
goal and the punishment she received from the government.

"Christabel, I want Dr. Strode to look after me. He was able to
give me the strength to continue living after all my hunger strikes.
Only he can help me now. Can you go and see him and tell him I
need him?"

Christabel leaves to visit Dr. Strode and Emmeline prepares to
revisit in her mind her second time as a prisoner in Holloway.

Emmeline and the Pethick-Lawrences are luckier than most
of the other suffragettes who end up in prison. They are well-
known and have a lot of influence with MPs and people with
political influence. The Home Secretary, who by this time
is Reginald McKenna, is put under so much pressure from
women's suffrage supporters, that he is forced to allow the
three leaders of the WSPU to move to the first division. They
are allowed to bring their own furniture into their cells, have
their own sheets and bed clothes. They can eat food prepared
by friends and family outside the prison. They are able to wear
their own clothes and read ooks and newspapers. It seems to
Emmeline that at long last the government has recognised their
status as political prisoners.

---

1 **life flashes before you** suddenly remember many events from your life – 3 **to relive** to experience sth again in your imagination – 8 **fierce** aggressive – 8 **a shadow of her former self** sb who is not as strong as they were in the past – 16 **to revisit** to return to an idea – 21 **to be put under pressure** to be forced by sb to do sth – 28 **at long last** finally

After a few days Emmeline asks one of the wardresses in the prison, "Are all our women now in the first division here in Holloway? I haven't seen any of them yet."

The wardress shakes her head, "No, it's only you and Mrs Pethick-Lawrence."

Emmeline is outraged. "We've been sitting here in comfort for days, while the rest of our women have been suffering solitary confinement, in cold, damp cells, dressed in filthy prison clothes, eating stale bread. This can't continue!"

And somehow the news starts to spread through the prison walls, from cell to cell, and eventually from prison to prison, that the government has once again betrayed suffragette women. In a few days, there are 80 women on hunger strike including Emmeline herself and the Pethick-Lawrences.

---

23 **outraged** feel angry and shocked – 25 **filthy** extremely dirty – 26 **stale** when food is old and hard

The screams of the strikers ring out along the corridors of Holloway as doctors take their long rubber tubes and funnels to each cell, force feeding the suffragette prisoners.

The hunger strike and force feeding of so many prisoners is in all the newspapers in Britain and the government is questioned continually about its cruel policy. But the Home Secretary sees things differently and is not very sympathetic to the hunger strikers.

"There is not one single prisoner who cannot leave prison this afternoon if they promise to stop their militant action".

The opposition MPs cannot believe what they are hearing. One labour member jumps up from his seat to reply.

"You are a disgrace! You call yourselves gentlemen and you force feed and murder women like this. You should be forced out of the government. This is the most disgraceful thing that has ever happened in the history of England. You will go down in history as the men who tortured innocent women."

Meanwhile, in Holloway, Emmeline Pankhurst listens in horror as the doctor's arrive at the cell next door to her where Mrs Pethick-Lawrence is locked up. There are screams and the sounds of a struggle and it is clear what is happening to her neighbour. Emmeline knows that she is next. What can she do? She has not eaten for several days and is very weak, but her anger at what they are doing gives her the strength that she needs. She jumps up out of bed as the door of her prison cell is thrown open and grabs a heavy water jug. Lifting it above her head with all the strength she has, she shouts, "If any of you come any closer, I WILL defend myself!"

The doctor and wardresses do not know what to do. This is not what they were expecting from a small 50-year-old woman who

---

1 **corridor** a long space in a building with doors that open into rooms – 13 **a disgrace** sth so bad or wrong that people find unacceptable – 16 **to go down in history** do sth important that will be remembered in the future – 17 **to torture** to hurt sb a lot in order to punish them or make them tell you information – 17 **innocent** not guilty of a crime

is weak from hunger and has been lying ill on her bed for the last few days. They leave Mrs Pankhurst's cell and do not try to force feed either her or Mrs Pethick-Lawrence again. In a man's prison, Mr Pethick-Lawrence is not as lucky as his wife, he is force fed twice a day for nearly ten days before he is released because he is so ill.

The government is now under so much pressure from the opposition and even their own supporters, that they know they cannot allow the situation to continue. If anyone dies as a result of being force fed, it will be very bad for the Liberals so, one by one, the prisoners are released.

The Prime Minister, Asquith has always been disliked by the WSPU, but now he and his government members are hated passionately, and they are about to become a target of increased militant suffragette action. Window breaking will seem like child's play in a few months.

When she leaves prison Emmeline is treated by her doctor, Dr Strode, and rests at home until she feels well enough to go to Paris to see Christabel, who has been leading the WSPU while everyone else was in jail.

"After what happened to us in prison and the reaction to the window breaking campaign, a lot of the other suffrage groups are saying that we should stop our militancy," Emmeline tells her daughter. "But I disagree. I think we've come too far to turn back now. The government hasn't been able to break us and even after the raid on our headquarters, the WSPU has continued to function – thanks to you. You've done an amazing job, Christabel, running everything from over here."

"We need to increase the pressure on the government. Asquith has broken every promise he's made about allowing women's suffrage bills time in Parliament. The only way is more force. We have to take even more militant action. Our war has to continue!

---

14 **a target** sth that an attack is directed at – 16 **child's play** sth that is easy to do – 26 **a raid** a surprise visit by the police looking for sth illegal

Why are men congratulated for their militant action, action that has actually caused people to die, but when women break windows to be given the right to vote, they are thrown in jail like common criminals and suffer the horror of force feeding?"

"It seems that the government cares far more for the security of property than for human life. Some of our supporters are already starting to go further - there was an arson attempt at the Home Secretary's office. I think this is the direction we have to move in, and we must make sure that the WSPU stays in control and coordinates all these militant acts. So, what I think we should do is publish a manifesto in 'Votes for Women' to tell the government exactly what's coming. They need to know that they're responsible for forcing us into more extreme action. It is time that Asquith and his government start to pay serious attention to us and if not, they'll have to deal with something much worse than what they've seen up to now."

Emmeline is woken up from her thoughts of the past by the arrival of Christabel, who is accompanied by a man pushing an empty wheelchair. The nurse follows them in, carrying a bag containing Emmeline's possessions.

"It's all arranged with Dr. Strode. He's going to treat you from now on and this gentleman is going to move you to another nursing home close to Dr Strode's house. The doctor will be on call and can get to the nursing home quickly whenever you need him, day or night."

After the journey in the ambulance through the busy streets of London, Emmeline is exhausted. Dr Strode is waiting for her in the new nursing home. When he sees her, a shadow passes over his face.

---

11 **manifesto** a document where sb says what their political or social objectives are – 14 **to pay attention to** to watch and listen to sb or sth – 23 **to be on call** to be available to work or make official visits when needed – 28 **a shadow passes over his face** his face changes to show a negative emotion eg sadness for a few seconds and then returns to normal

"Emmeline! I'm so sorry to see you look so unwell. You should have come to me earlier; I am your doctor after all. But, you're here with me now and we'll see what we can do to make you feel better."

"I want my stomach pumped, Doctor. I have this awful nausea all the time. The same as I had after my hunger strikes. Your treatment gave me the strength to carry on all those years ago. I don't think anything else is going to work now."

Dr. Strode shakes his head sadly, "Emmeline, my dear. I can't do that to you. You're far too weak – it would kill you. No, you need a different type of treatment. Once you've made yourself comfortable, I'll come back and examine you properly."

After the doctor has left, Emmeline starts to lose herself to her memories again.

'Things were so different after I came back from Paris. We published our manifesto, but the new period of militancy didn't go down well with everyone in the WSPU. I was right to do what I did, wasn't I? What choice did I have? I couldn't allow any disunity in the WSPU – they all had to go, Sylvia, Adela, the Pethick-Lawrences. Our campaign was everything. Christabel and I gave our lives to it. The others, they just didn't have the same commitment. They wanted other things.'

Although the WSPU's aim was to enfranchise women so they could vote in elections, the union itself has slowly moved away from the democracy of its early days. Once they moved into their London headquarters, Emmeline and Christabel had been able to take more control over the running of the organisation. New members had to sign a declaration of loyalty to the union

---

5 **to have your stomach pumped** to have the contents of your stomach removed by a tube through your mouth – 13 **to lose yourself to sth** to think about one thing so much that you forget about everything else – 17 **to go down well** to be popular – 19 **disunity** when people in a group don't agree with each other – 22 **commitment** giving your time and energy to sth that you believe in – 25 **democracy** a political system where people choose who rules them by voting for them in elections – 28 **declaration of loyalty** officially saying that you will support one organisation and not any others

and were not allowed to work for any other political party until women's suffrage was passed. Christabel then announced that the WSPU's annual conference would be cancelled and that all the important decisions would be made by her, Emmeline and a committee that they would choose. Shortly after this, in 1907, seventy-seven WSPU members decided to leave and form a new suffrage organisation, the Women's Freedom League, which would focus on getting the vote for women through non-violent action.

The publication of the manifesto marks the end of the six-year relationship between the Pethick- Lawrences and Emmeline and Christabel. After their terrible experience of being imprisoned and force fed, both Mr and Mrs Pethick-Lawrence are unhappy with the way things are going. They are not sure that the end justifies the means. They do not want to be part of arson attacks where someone could actually be killed and end up in jail for conspiracy to murder, so they leave the WSPU. It is not clear to many people whether they leave voluntarily or are forced out by Emmeline and Christabel. The WSPU moves to a new headquarters and starts a different newspaper, 'The Suffragette', edited by Christabel in Paris.

Attacks on Asquith become more frequent. On a visit to Dublin, he finds suffragettes waiting for him at every corner. There are suffragettes ready to confront him on trains, on the boat across the Irish sea, at political meetings where he is speaking, at every public appearance he makes, someone even throws a hatchet at his car as he leaves Dublin. There is an attempted arson attack at the theatre when he goes to see a performance of a play. The suffragettes responsible make sure to wait until everyone has left the building before they try to set fire to it.

---

12 **to be imprisoned** to be sent to prison – 14 **the end justifies the means** the final objective is so important that you can use any action you need even if it is bad – 18 **voluntarily** because you want to do sth – 24 **to confront** to stand in front of sb in order to fight or argue with them – 27 **a hatchet** a tool used to cut wood

'We chose symbols of the male British establishment to attack,' remembers Emmeline. 'They got so upset when we started attacking golf courses. I wish I'd seen their faces when we burnt Votes for Women into the grass with acid and changed the flags in the holes for WSPU flags. And we followed poor Emily's example, and started setting fire to letter boxes. I really thought our campaign had worked when Asquith announced a new franchise bill at the end of the year. What a fool - I should never have called a truce then! Asquith was never going to allow women to get a vote! After that Christabel and I decided that enough was enough – that it was time to discredit the government in the eyes of the world. To show that English law was a failure. To spoil English sports, to hurt businesses, to destroy valuable property and to demoralise society. We believed that the English people would tell the government to stop our action but the only way it could be stopped was by giving women the vote.'

It is February 1913 and Asquith and Reginald McKenna, the Home Secretary, are extremely worried about the WSPU and Emmeline Pankhurst. McKenna is listing the attacks the suffragettes have carried out so far:

"Apart from their attacks on golf courses and post boxes, they've cut telephone and telegraph wires. In one instance they succeeded in cutting communications between London and Glasgow for hours.

They've smashed the windows of greenhouses in Kew Gardens and burnt down an orchid house there, destroying rare tropical

---

9 **to call a truce** to agree to stop fighting – 11 **enough is enough** you want sth to stop – 13 **a failure** not successful – 14 **to demoralise** make sb lose confidence and want to stop doing sth – 22 **post box** metal box where you put letters you want to be sent for delivery – 23 **telegraph** a way of sending messages before the telephone was invented – 23 **wires** long thin metal pieces which carry electrical signals – 26 **greenhouse** a glass building used for growing plants – 26 **Kew Gardens** a famous botanical gardens in London – 27 **to burn down** to be destroyed by fire – 27 **orchid** a plant with coloured flowers with unusual shapes

flowers. And, I don't know how they did it, but they even
managed to smash a jewel case at the Tower of London."

"And now this bomb at Lloyd George's country house," Asquith
adds. "If all those other things weren't bad enough!"

"It was very lucky the Chancellor of the Exchequer wasn't
there."

"Can we be sure that it was the suffragettes who planted the
bomb? No-one saw anything, I understand."

"The police found a hat pin and a hair pin near the house, so it
looks like it was one of Mrs Pankhurst's women. Ultimately, she is
responsible for all of this. We need to arrest her and lock her up
for a very long time," McKenna replies.

"Hopefully, this new bill we're about to pass will help with
that. We've got enough to worry about with the problems in
Ireland, Europe and the British Empire. We need to sort out this
suffragette problem once and for all – these women are no longer
a minor inconvenience."

The new bill Asquith's government passes, to try and stop the
effectiveness of the suffragette hunger strikes, becomes known as
the 'Cat and Mouse Act' and Emmeline is about to experience it
first-hand. The law says that when a hunger striker is in danger of
dying, they can be released temporarily to recover, but then they
have to return to prison to continue their sentence. McKenna has
the police arrest Emmeline Pankhurst for conspiracy to damage
property once again. In the trial, the prosecution argue successfully
that Mrs Pankhurst has full control over the violent action of the
WSPU. She is found guilty and, to the shock of her supporters in
the courtroom, Emmeline is sentenced to three years in jail and the
game of cat and mouse begins.

---

2 **the Tower of London** a historical castle in central London – 9 **pin** a thin piece of metal
with a point at the end used to keep sth in position – 16 **once and for all** for the last time
– 17 **a minor inconvenience** a small problem – 19 **effectiveness** working well – 21 **first-
hand** directly – 25 **the prosecution** the lawyers responsible for proving in a law court that
sb is guilty of a crime – 27 **to be found guilty** when a court decides you committed a
crime

How many times did they release me from prison and then rearrest me when they thought I'd had enough time to recover? Emmeline asks herself. If Dr Strode hadn't looked after me so well, I would have died in 1913. If the war hadn't started and I'd had to finish my prison sentence, perhaps that would have been the end of me.

Emmeline can faintly hear Christabel calling her name from a long way away, but she is lost in what might be regrets.

We made so many sacrifices that year, she thinks sadly. That was the year poor Emily died at the Epsom Derby. And the year my family ruptured. Would I do everything all over again if I had the chance? If I'd known that the war would change everything and that's what would give us the vote, perhaps…

It is growing dark now and the memories are starting to fade but a final image of Christabel, Sylvia and Adela as little children playing on the beach makes Emmeline smile as she drifts off into a deep sleep. The last thing she is aware of is a man's voice saying, "It won't be long now" and someone holding her hand and kissing her softly on her cheek.

How did the WSPU change after the manifesto was published?

What was the 'Cat and Mouse Act'?

7 **faintly** not clearly – 8 **regrets** feelings of sadness about sth you did and wish you could change – 9 **to make a sacrifice** to give up sth important so you can do or have another thing that you think is more important – 10 **the Epsom Derby** a famous horse race in England – 11 **to rupture** to end good relations between people – 14 **to fade** to become less clear and start to disappear

Think about it...

Do you think the end always justifies the means? Why/why not?

If you were Emmeline Pankhurst, would you regret your actions? Why/why not?

Background information

What happened to…?

…Sylvia and Adela Pankhurst

There was always rivalry between the Pankhurst sisters,
especially as it was obvious that Emmeline always preferred
Christabel. Sylvia and Adela Pankhurst were dedicated to the
suffragette cause and spent time in prison and on hunger strikes
but, unlike their mother and older sister, they were also socialists
and wanted to help working class people, both men and women,
improve their conditions.

Sylvia worked with other political organisations such as the
Labour Party, which annoyed Christabel in particular. For
Christabel, the WSPU was a women-only organisation and
members should be completely dedicated to the suffragette cause.
Sylvia was not in favour of the campaign of violence and was
worried that so many WSPU were leaving the organisation as
a result. In November 1913 she tried unsuccessfully to take the
leadership of the WSPU from Christabel, who was still living
in Paris to avoid police arrest. In answer to her betrayal of her
older sister, Sylvia was thrown out of the WSPU in January 1914.
Sylvia's later interest in communism and her decision to live
and have a child with her partner Silvio Erasmus Corio, without
marrying him caused more problems in her relationship with
Emmeline and Christabel.

Later in life, Sylvia became friends with Haile Selassie, the
Emperor of Ethiopia. In 1956 after the death of her partner, Sylvia
took her son, Richard, to live in Addis Ababa in Ethiopia. She
died there in 1960 aged 78.

When Sylvia was told to leave the WSPU, Emmeline became
worried that Adela would start working with Sylvia against

---

4 **rivalry** a serious and continuing competition between two people or groups –
18 **leadership** position of being in control of a group of people – 21 **communism** political
and social system where everyone is equal and worker's control production

Christabel. The fight between Sylvia and Christabel was very public and Emmeline did not want any more negative news about problems in her family, so in February 1914 she sent Adela to Australia with £20 and some warm clothes. Adela never saw her mother again.

Adela helped start the communist party of Australia but became very right-wing over the years, even leading an organisation which supported fascism during World War II. She died in Sydney in 1961 aged 75.

…Christabel Pankhurst?

When the vote was given to a limited number of women in 1918, Christabel decided to stand as a Member of Parliament in the general election. She was defeated by the Labour Party candidate by only 775 votes. In 1921 she moved to the United States and became very religious, joining different evangelistic Christian groups. She died in California in 1958, aged 77.

…Emily Wilding Davison?

Emily Wilding Davison is probably one of the most infamous British suffragettes even if a lot of people do not remember her name. On 4th June 1913, she ran out in front of King George V's horse at the Epsom Derby, a prestigious English horse race attended by thousands of spectators. The horse hit her and she was knocked unconscious. Emily died 4 days later from a fractured skull. There is still a lot of debate about what she was trying to do. Some people think she was trying to attach a WSPU flag to the horse, others believe she was trying to kill herself.

---

7 **right-wing** supporting the ideas of political parties on the right who believe in keeping traditional customs and values – 8 **fascism** political and social system where the government has strong control of society and the economy and does not allow political opposition – 13 **to stand (as an MP) to** compete in an election (to become a member of parliament) – 16 **evangelistic** describing a religious group that tries to persuade people to become Christians – 24 **spectators** people watching a sports event – 25 **unconscious** in a state similar to sleep but caused by a serious injury – 26 **fractured skull** when the bones of your head are broken

Whatever her intention, Emily became the first person to die for votes for women and she became an instant martyr for the WSPU. The Epsom Derby was actually filmed that day and the newsreel of the moment when Emily was knocked down was shown at cinemas up and down the country.

On the day of Emily's funeral 5,000 women marched behind her coffin and over 50,000 people watched the procession on the street. Emmeline had been released from prison for 15 days so she could recover from hunger strike. Although she was still very weak, she was determined to attend the funeral, but as soon as Emmeline left her flat, she was arrested again and sent back to Holloway prison under the Cat and Mouse Act.

There is a plaque commemorating Emily Wilding Davison inside a broom cupboard in the House of Commons. During the night of the 1911 census, Emily hid illegally in this cupboard so she could record 'The House of Commons' as her address in the census document. The plaque was put up by an MP without permission because he was angry that the statues in Parliament did not celebrate people who actually believed in democracy.

…The Pethick-Lawrences?

After they left the WSPU, the Pethick-Lawrences continued to campaign for women's suffrage and started the United Suffragists, which was open to men and women. They also continued to edit 'Votes for Women', but now as an independent publication.

Frederick Pethick-Lawrence was elected as an MP for the Labour Party 1923-1931 and 1935-1947.

Emmeline died in 1954 aged 86. Frederick married another ex-suffragette in 1957 and died in 1961 aged 89.

---

4 **newsreel** a short film of news that people watched in the cinema in the past – 7 **coffin** a box for a dead person's body to be buried or burned in – 13 **plaque** a flat piece of metal or other material with writing on that is attached to a door or wall – 13 **to commemorate** to remind people of an important event or person from the past – 14 **broom cupboard** a place where cleaning materials are kept – 15 **census** an official count to record the number of people living in a country and their ages and jobs

The First World War and votes for women

When the war started, the WSPU stopped its militant action and all suffragette prisoners were released from prison.

With so many men fighting in the war between 1914 and 1918, around two million women were needed to do the jobs that that were now empty – jobs in manufacturing and agriculture. Women also worked in armament factories making weapons, became auxiliaries in the army in non-combat roles and volunteered as nurses looking after injured soldiers.

By the end of the war, it was obvious that women were capable of doing things that were traditionally done by men and society's opinion of gender roles changed significantly. Even Herbert Asquith changed his mind about giving women the votes, but by 1918 he was no longer Prime Minister.

Suffragette memorabilia and photographs

You can see a collection of suffragette memorabilia and photographs from the Museum of London online.

https://artsandculture.google.com/partner/museum-of-london

The Ladies' Gallery in the House of Commons

Women were banned from the public galleries of the House of Commons in 1778 and the only way they could watch parliamentary debates before 1834 was either to disguise themselves as men or, if they had friends in the Commons, climb up to the attic, where they could look down through the ceiling from a handful of small windows around a ventilation shaft. The shaft was built to extract the heat, smoke and stale air from the

---

6 **manufacturing** the business of producing goods in large numbers – 6 **agriculture** farming – 7 **armament factory** a place where guns and bombs etc are made – 7 **weapon** an object used in fighting or war eg guns, knives – 8 **auxiliary** sb who is employed to help other people in their work – 8 **non-combat** not involved in fighting – 12 **gender roles** traditional responsibilities based on whether a person is male or female – 22 **to be banned** to officially say sth must not be done – 24 **to disguise yourself** to hange your appearance so other people will not know who you are – 26 **attic** the room at the top of a building under the roof – 28 **shaft** a long vertical space eg for a lift – 28 **stale air** not fresh or new

chamber of the House of Commons into the attic space. Even though it must have been very hot, smelly and uncomfortable, women still came to listen. After a fire in 1834 destroyed the building, the Houses of Parliament were rebuilt and a special Ladies' Gallery was included. The Ladies' Gallery was given the nickname 'The Cage' because metal grilles were put over the windows so the MPs would not be distracted by women watching them.

It was very difficult for women in the Gallery to see through the grilles and they were very unpopular. Millicent Fawcett (leader of the National Union of Women's Suffrage Societies – the NUWSS) wrote "…it was like using a gigantic pair of spectacles which did not fit and made the Ladies' Gallery a grand place for getting headaches." On 25 April 1906, Annie Kenney and Sylvia Pankhurst were thrown out of the Ladies' Gallery by the police after hitting their hands against the grille and shouting 'Votes for Women'. On 28th October 1908, two suffragists from the Women's Freedom League, chained and padlocked themselves to the grille. The authorities had to remove the grille from the window, still attached to the women, in order to cut through the chains. After this incident, the Engineer's Department in the House of Commons, bought some bolt clippers, so they could easily cut through anymore chains and padlocks in the future. The clippers are still kept in the office of the Principal Doorkeeper.

---

2 **smelly** with a bad smell – 6 **nickname** an informal name for sb – 6 **cage** a structure made from metal where animals or birds are kept – 6 **grille** a metal frame used to cover sth eg a window or machine as protection – 18 **to chain** to tie with metal chains – 18 **padlock** a block of metal with a U-shaped bar which opens with a key and can be used to fasten things together – 22 **bolt clippers** a tool used for cutting chains or padlocks

Activities

Focus on the story

1. What happened and when?

Put these WSPU actions in the order that they happened. Write the number in the column on the left-hand side. The first one has been done as an example.

order	action
	Mary Leigh and Edith New throw stones through Asquith's window when he is Prime Minister.
	WSPU members start to disrupt political meetings around the country.
	WSPU supporters smash shop windows in London in an hour-long campaign.
	A WSPU supporter plants a bomb at Lloyd George's country house.
	300 WSPU women march to Caxton Hall on the day the new Liberal government's legislative plan is announced.
	Emily Wilding Davison sets fire to a letter box at Parliament Street Post Office.
	A group of women go to protest outside Asquith's house when he is the Chancellor of the Exchequer.
	500,000 people meet in Hyde Park to support women's suffrage.
	A suffragette throws a hatchet at Asquith's car.
1	Annie Kenney and Christabel Pankhurst ask Liberal Party candidates if they will give women the vote at a meeting in Manchester.
	Hundreds of WSPU supporters break the windows of government offices.
	80 suffragettes, including Emmeline Pankhurst, go on hunger strike at the same time.
	'Votes for Women' is started.
	Marion Wallace Dunlop goes on hunger strike.
	Emmeline and 11 other women march to Parliament to test the Tumultuous Petitions Act.

2. Why is the place so important?

Write a sentence to explain why these places are important in the story. The first one has been done as an example.

Manchester

Emmeline was born in Manchester. Manchester is also important because it's where Annie Kenney and Christabel Pankhurst asked the Liberal Party about votes for women.

Caxton Hall

_____

_____

Parliament/the House of Commons

_____

_____

Clement's Inn

_____

_____

Holloway Prison

_____

_____

Hyde Park

_____

_____

10 Downing Street

_____

_____

Paris

_____

_____

3. How does the sentence end?

Cross out the incorrect option(s). There could be more than one.

1. The suffragettes publicised their campaigns by…
a. …writing chalk message on the pavement.
b. …writing about them in a newspaper.
c. …ringing on doorbells.
d. …putting up posters.

2. The newspaper 'Votes for Women'…
a. …cost a shilling.
b. …was printed in the Pethick-Lawrence's house.
c. …was sold in shops.
d. …always had a picture of Emmeline on the cover.

3. In Holloway prison…
a. …prisoners wore special prison clothes.
b. …the cells were small and dry.
c. …prisoners could not exercise outside.
d. …there were three different divisions.

4. On Women's Sunday…
a. …everyone was given a WSPU tea set.
b. …people came from all over the country.
c. …only women were allowed to march.
d. …the military took control.

5. In the UK in 1918…
a. …there was finally universal suffrage.
b. …all men aged 21 and over could vote.
c. …all women aged 30 and over could vote.
c. …women did not have the same rights as men.

Focus on the people

1. What are they like?

Match the words or phrases in the box to the correct person.
There are five for each person. The first one has been done as an
example.

---

1. oldest   2. wealthy   3. works with other political parties

4. studied law   5. arch-enemy   6. artistic

7. excellent fundraiser   8. favourite

9. breaks his promise   10. edits the first WSPU newspaper

11. WSPU target

12. pacifist   13. is always true to the WSPU motto

14. political reformer

15. doesn't believe the end justifies the means   16. socialist

17. religious   18. efficient organiser

19. disgraces the Pankhurst family name   20. anti-suffragette

---

Christabel _1_ ___ ___ ___ ___
Emmeline Pethick-Lawrence ___ ___ ___ ___ ___

Sylvia _   __ ___ ___ ___ ___
Herbert Henry Asquith ___ ___ ___ ___ ___

2. Describe the characters

Now complete the texts below with the words or phrases from
activity 1.

Christabel is Emmeline Pankhurst's [1]_____ daughter. She is also her [2]_____ which causes problems between Christabel and Sylvia. Christabel [3]_____ at Manchester University but because she was a woman, she could not become a lawyer. Christabel [4]_____, 'Deeds, not words' and is the most militant of the Pankhurst sisters. In later life, Christabel becomes very [5]_____ and goes to live in the United States.

Sylvia is Emmeline's second oldest child. She studied at the Royal College of Art and is very [6]_____. She designs the banners, posters and jewellery for the WSPU. She is a dedicated suffragette and also a [7]_____ - she wants working class men and women to get the vote too. Christabel believes that Sylvia has betrayed the WSPU because she [8]_____, including the Labour Party. Sylvia is a [9]_____ and does not believe in violence and is worried about the militancy of her mother and older sister. She is forced to leave the WSPU in 1913. After the war, Sylvia [10]_____ when she has a son out of wedlock with an Italian anarchist.

Emmeline Pethick-Lawrence is a [11]_____ supporter of women's suffrage. The WSPU use her house in Clement's Inn as their headquarters in London. Mrs Pethick-Lawrence is an [12]_____ and has a lot of good ideas for raising money for the WSPU. She starts and [13]_____, 'Votes for Women', which is sold around the country. She is also an [14]_____ and it is thanks to her that Women's Sunday is so successful. However, Mrs Pethick-Lawrence [15]_____ and leaves the WSPU when the suffragettes become more militant.

Herbert Henry Asquith, the Liberal Party Prime Minister, is the WSPU's political opponent and Emmeline's Pankhurst's ^{16.}_____. Although he is a ^{17.}_____ and his government wants to give the vote to more men, he does not want to enfranchise women. He promises supporters of votes for women that he will allow private member's bills to be discussed in Parliament but then he ^{18.}_____. Because his is ^{19.}_____ , he becomes a ^{20.}_____ - women throw stones through his windows and even set fire to a theatre he goes to.

3. What was Emmeline Pankhurst like?

Now write a short paragraph about **Emmeline Pankhurst**.

4. What was their name?

Write the name of these people who also appear in the story.

1. Emmeline Pankhurst's youngest daughter:

   _____

2. Emmeline's husband: _____

3. Emmeline's adopted daughter: _____

4. Emmeline's doctor: _____

5. A Labour MP and friend of Sylvia: _____

6. Sylvia's son: _____

7. Two important WSPU members: _____
   and _____

8. Two WSPU members who threw stones:
   _____ and _____

9. The first hunger striker: _____

10. The first arsonist: _____

11. Two Home Secretaries: _____ and
    _____

Focus on grammar

Present perfect simple

Look at this sentence from the start of the story which uses the **present perfect**:

> *Emmeline Pankhurst has been many things in her life.*

Can you remember the things that Emmeline has been?

1. Structure

To form the **present perfect** we use **have/has + past participle** (pp).

positive	negative	question
I / you / we / they have + pp (I've etc)	I / you / we / they haven't + pp	Have you + pp?
he / she / it has + pp (She's etc)	he / she / it hasn't + pp	Has she + pp?

If a verb is regular the past participle is the **-ed** form. e.g. Emmeline **has lived** in Manchester, London and the United States.

There are a lot of irregular verbs in the story. Complete the table with the past participle for each verb. The first one has been done as an example.

verb (to…)	past participle	verb (to…)	past participle
1. be	been	11. hear	
2. break		12. hide	
3. bring		13. know	
4. come / become		14. leave	
5. cost		15. lose	
6. do		16. make	
7. eat		17. see	
8. fight		18. take	
9. go		19. tell	
10. have		20. write	

2. Use

We can use the **present perfect**…

- to talk about a period of time that starts in the past and continues until now (e.g. recently, so far, in the last few days.)

Emmeline Pankhurst has been many things in her life.

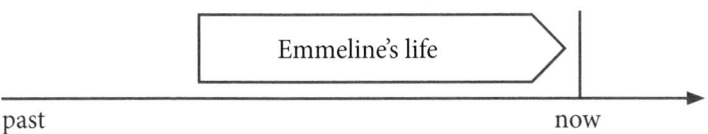

past   now

- with today / this morning / this week / this year etc when these periods are not finished.

There have been four by-elections this year.

- with **for** if we want to say how long we have done something.
Emmeline Pankhurst has been a suffragette for 56 years.

- with **since** if we want to say when the activity started.
Emmeline Pankhurst has been a suffragette since she was 14.

- to talk about an action that happened in the past but has a result now.
A large crowd has gathered to watch the march.

The people gathered before the march started (an action in the past). They are there watching the march **now**.

- with **just** to talk about something that happened a short time ago.
I've just heard that the government hasn't included votes for women on their agenda.

- with **already** to show that something happened before now or before you expected.
The police search railway stations and ports trying to find Christabel but they are too late - Christabel has already made her way safely across the English Channel…

Note: just and already go between has/have and the main verb.

- with **yet** in <u>negatives</u> and <u>questions</u> to show that something has not happened, but you are expecting it to happen.
Are all our women now in the first division here in Holloway?
I haven't seen any of them yet.

 Note: *Yet* goes at the end of the sentence.

3. Practice

1. Match the time expressions from the box with for and since. The first two have been done as examples.

> 1. ~~half past ten~~   2. ~~30 minutes~~   3. 1900
> 4. the First World War   5. a quarter of an hour
> 6. the morning   7. several days   8. 30 years
> 9. a very long time   10. she was in prison
> 11. several months   12. the King's Speech
> 13. as long as she can remember   14. spring

for	since
30 minutes	half past ten

2. For spaces **1-5** change the verb in brackets into the **present perfect**. For spaces **a-e** choose one of the time expressions from the previous exercise.

1. Emmeline ^{1.}_____ (fight) for women's suffrage for ^{a.}_____.

2. The prisoners are on hunger strike and they ^{2.}_____(not eat) for ^{b.}_____.

3. Emmeline ^{3.}_____ (have) stomach problems since ^{c.}_____.

4. Christabel ^{4.}_____ (be) in Paris
   since ^{d.}_____.

5. Sylvia and Keir Hardie ^{5.} _____
   (know) each other for ^{e.}_____.

3. Look at Mrs Pethick-Lawrence's to do list below and write
   sentences in the **present perfect** to say what WSPU members
   have already done and what they haven't done yet. There are
   two example sentences.

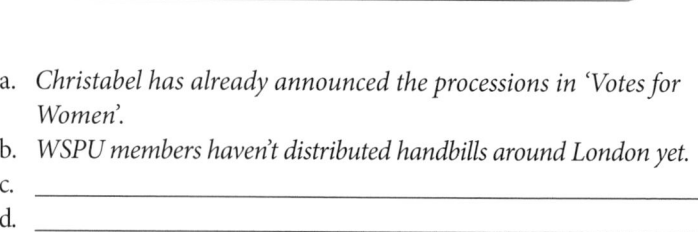

Women's Sunday to do list

- *announce processions in 'Votes for Women' (Christabel)*
- *design handbills and posters (Sylvia)*
- *put up posters in shop windows (Sylvia and Annie)*
- *distribute handbills around London (WSPU members)*
- *chalk announcements on pavements (WSPU members)*
- *book trains into London (Frederick)*
- *make purple, white and green rosettes (the Pankhurst sisters)*

a. *Christabel has already announced the processions in 'Votes for Women'.*
b. *WSPU members haven't distributed handbills around London yet.*
c. _____
d. _____
e. _____

f. _____

g. _____

4. Write the words in the correct order to make questions or instructions (Q) and then, using the **present perfect**, write down your answer (A) to each question on the line provided. You have been given the first word of each questions to help.

1. how / town or city / lived / in / long / current / you / have / your
   Q: How _____?
   A: _____

2. write down / Emmeline Pankhurst / just / something / learnt / about / have / that / you
   Q: Write down _____
   A: _____

3. what / so / you / DELTA readers / far/ read / other / have
   Q: What_____?
   A: _____

4. is there / but you should have / important / anything / done / today / that / you / haven't
   Q: Is there _____?
   A: _____

5. have / activity / yet / you / questions / the / in / finished / this / all
   Q: Have _____?
   A: _____

Build your vocabulary

Focus on words and phrases

1. Odd one out

Find the odd one out (the one that is different to the others) in each group and say why. The first one has been done as an example. You can use the glossary to help you.

1. a. legislation   b. a petition   c. a bill   d. an act

Why? *A petition is when a member of the public asks the government to do something. The others are connected to laws that the governments make.*

2. a. Chancellor of the Exchequer   b. Home Secretary
    c. Prime Minister   d. House of Commons

Why? _____

3. a. a wife   b. a widow   c. a social reformer   d. a mother

Why? _____

4. a. radical   b. mounted   c. undercover   d. plain clothes

Why? _____

5. a. arson   b. assault   c. burn down   d. set fire to

Why? _____

6. a. handbill   b. pamphlet   c. motto   d. poster

Why? _____

7. a. opponent   b. ally   c. arch-enemy   d. rival

Why? _____

2. Word search

Can you find the 15 words hidden in the puzzle? Write the word next to the definition and then draw a line through the word when you have found it in the word search. The words can be horizontal, vertical or diagonal and some could be written backwards.

1. a long piece of material with a message written on it
   _____

2. pay money as a punishment for breaking a rule/ law
   _____

3. walk together in order to protest against or support something
   _____

4. make stronger
   _____

5. speak very quietly so only the person close to you can hear
   _____

6. dark marks on your skin when you have been hit by something
   _____

7. the same rights for everyone in society
   _____

8. objective/purpose
   _____

9. a short sentence that says what an organisation believes
   _____

10. a short sentence used to advertise an idea or product
    _____

11. the right to vote in political elections
    _____

12. extremely dirty
    _____

13. being responsible for something bad that has happened
    _____

14. move your head down and then up
    _____

15. become very weak or die because you do not have enough food to eat
    _____

D	E	D	G	B	N	S	S	Y	T	S	R
H	O	S	X	O	L	O	T	Q	U	S	E
N	C	W	I	O	A	L	R	F	Y	T	N
U	C	R	G	U	I	L	F	E	H	R	N
F	E	A	A	U	R	R	U	Q	T	E	A
Z	N	Q	G	M	A	B	C	U	L	N	B
R	Q	B	W	G	I	R	A	A	I	G	D
W	X	C	E	D	J	R	X	L	F	T	E
E	V	R	A	T	S	I	C	I	P	H	P
E	W	H	I	S	P	E	R	T	L	E	U
I	E	N	I	F	D	V	C	Y	U	N	V
M	O	T	T	O	B	F	I	M	U	G	R

3. Which word is correct?

Choose the correct word to complete the sentences.

At the end of her life Emmeline Pankhurst was living in a nursing house / home.

Mrs Pankhurst was a thorn in the side / back of the Liberal Government.

The Pankhursts never took the easy way in / out and were often sent to jail.

The King's Debate / Speech is on the opening day of Parliament.

Before a suffrage march the WSPU members worked around the clock / hours publicising the event.

The pouring snow / rain didn't stop the suffragettes from marching.

The newspaper burst into ashes / flames when Emmeline threw it on the fire.

Emmeline Pankhurst – the mind map

Make your own mind map of words connected to the story.
Think of words to add to each topic area. You can add your own
topic areas too.

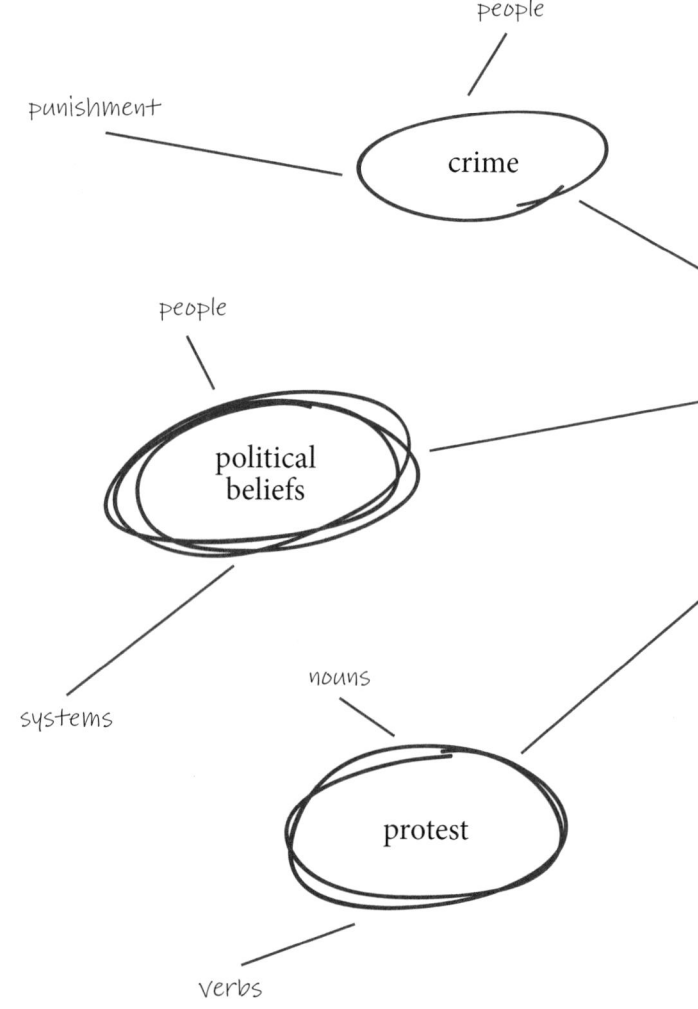

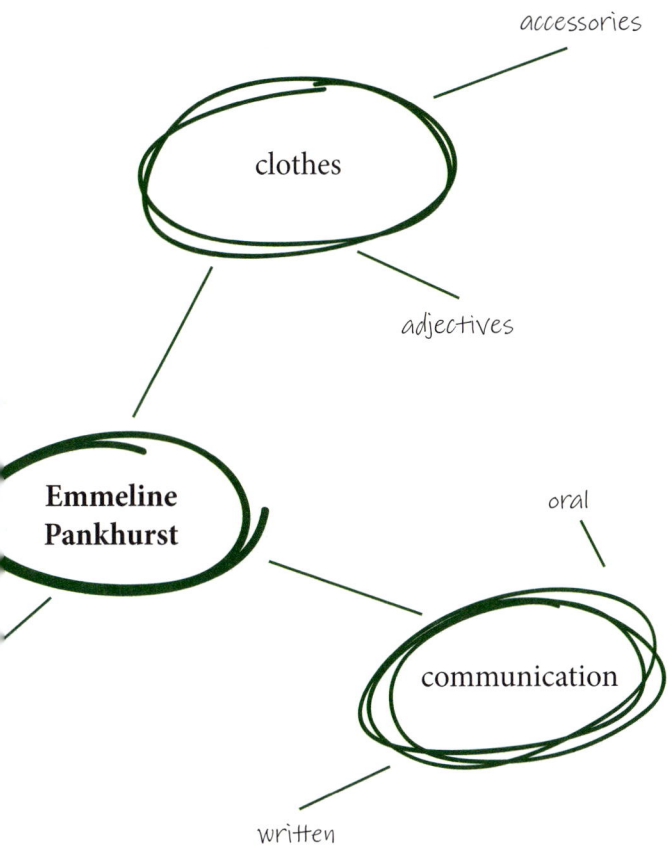

accessories

clothes

adjectives

Emmeline
Pankhurst

oral

communication

written

Compare your words with the words on the next pages. Did you include some of the same words? Tick the words you know and look back at the text and explanations to check the meanings of any new words. You can add your own words and notes to the glossary like the examples.

Political glossary

THE SUFFRAGETTES GET WILDER DAILY
& SMASH SHOP WINDOWS ON 30 GAILS

An **Act of Parliament** is a law. All Acts start as bills.

An **amendment** is a change to a bill which is proposed by an MP or a member of the House of Lords.

A **bill** is a proposal for a new law or a significant change to an existing law. To become law, a bill goes through different processes in Parliament. A bill is read and debated several times and amendments can be made. After each debate MPs vote to see if the bill can pass to the next stage.

A **by-election** is an election that takes place if a seat in the House of Commons becomes vacant before there is a General Election.

Candidate somebody who would like to be voted for

The **Chancellor of the Exchequer** is the government's finance minister.

To **disenfranchise** (verb) (**disenfranchisement** - noun) to take away the right to vote.

The **electorate** are all the people who are allowed to vote.

to enfranchise (verb) (**enfranchisement** - noun) to give somebody the right to vote in an election.

A **general election** is when the voters of the country elect Members of Parliament (MPs) to the House of Commons.

The **Home Secretary** is a senior position in the UK government (the interior minister in other countries). The Home Secretary is responsible for law enforcement, national security and, in the past, prisons.

House of Commons is where Members of Parliament represent the interests of the UK public.

House of Lords is the second chamber of the UK Parliament. It's members are not elected by the public.

The King's Speech is the speech the King reads on the opening of Parliament. It announces the programme of legislation that the Government want to introduce over the parliamentary year.

Legislation (noun) (**to legislate** verb) is a law suggested by the Government and made official by Parliament.

A **Member of Parliament (MP)** is the person elected by voters in a particular area to represent them in the House of Commons.

Parliament in the UK is made up of the Crown (the King or Queen), the House of Lords and the House of Commons.

A **petition** is a formal written request sent to Parliament by members of the public asking the Government for some type of action.

The Prime Minister (PM) is the leader of the Government. They live at 10 Downing Street in London.

Private Members' Bills are introduced by individual MPs and not the Government. Very few become law but they can create publicity about a particular issue.

Public Galleries are areas where members of the public can watch proceedings in the House of Commons or the House of Lords.

Representation of the People Act was a law passed in 1918. One of the changes it made was to allow women aged 30 and over, who occupied a house or were married to a man who did, to vote in general elections.

Suffrage is the right to vote in political elections.

Vote / to vote is the right to give your opinion in an election, usually by filling in a paper with the names of candidates.

Glossary

	New word?	Notes / connected words
Crime		
assault	☐	
be banned	☐	
be force fed	☐	
be found guilty	☐	
be imprisoned	☐	
be sentenced	☐	
beat	☐	
cell	☐	
conspire	☐	
courtroom	☐	
disorderly conduct	☐	
hooligans	☐	
illegal	☐	
incite violence	☐	
innocent	☐	
mounted police	☐	
on the charge of	☐	
pay a fine	☐	
plain clothes police	☐	
prosecution	☐	
prosecutor	☐	
solitary confinement	☐	
raid	☐	
ruffian	☐	
take the blame	☐	
torture	☐	
undercover police	☐	
witness	☐	
Fire		
arson	☐	

	New word?	Notes / connected words
ashes	☐	
burn down	☐	
burst into flames	☐	
set fire to	☐	

Political beliefs & systems

anarchist	☐
cause	☐
communism	☐
conservative	☐
democracy	☐
equality	☐
fascism	☐
goal	☐
left-wing	☐
martyr	☐
opponent	☐
oppression	☐
pacifism	☐
radical	☐
right-wing	☐
rival	☐
rivalry	☐
social reformer	☐
socialism	☐
stay true to sth	☐

Protest

address a meeting	☐
admit defeat	☐
block	☐
call a truce	☐
campaign	☐

	New word?	Notes / connected words
confront	☐	
deed	☐	
demonstration	☐	
deputation	☐	
direct action	☐	
disobey	☐	
disrupt	☐	
distraction	☐	
disturbance	☐	
heckle	☐	
hunger striker	☐	
incite	☐	
march	☐	
militancy	☐	
militant	☐	
obstruction	☐	
procession	☐	
put under pressure	☐	
resort to	☐	
rowdy	☐	
shout sb down	☐	
smash	☐	
spectacle	☐	
spectators	☐	
strike	☐	
struggle	☐	
symbol	☐	
tactics	☐	
take to the streets	☐	
talk a bill out	☐	
the end justifies the means	☐	
turn out	☐	
unite	☐	

	New word?	Notes / connected words

Managing an organisation

	New word?
agenda	☐
board	☐
commitment	☐
dedicate yourself to sth	☐
make a sacrifice	☐
Executive Committee	☐
fundraiser	☐
headquarters	☐
leadership	☐
priorities	☐
put a plan together	☐
raise money	☐
recruit	☐
registrar	☐
take over	☐
work around the clock	☐

Communication

	New word?
agenda	☐
banner	☐
command	☐
debate	☐
declare	☐
distribute	☐
edit	☐
edition	☐
extract	☐
groan	☐
handbill	☐
manifesto	☐
motto	☐
mutter	☐

	New word?	Notes / connected words
newsagent's	☐	
newsreel	☐	
pamphlet	☐	
plaque	☐	
printing press	☐	
publicise	☐	
shut up	☐	
sigh	☐	
slogan	☐	
subscription	☐	
whisper	☐	
word for word	☐	

Clothes, accessories

apron	☐	
badge	☐	
bow	☐	
bun	☐	
embroidered	☐	
hair pin	☐	
hat pin	☐	
in your Sunday best	☐	
lace	☐	
outfit	☐	
ribbon	☐	
sash	☐	
shapeless	☐	
stamped	☐	
stockings	☐	
veiled hat	☐	
wide-brimmed hat	☐	
woollen	☐	

	New word?	Notes / connected words
Appearance		
burly	☐	
disguise yourself	☐	
elegant	☐	
eye-catching	☐	
frail	☐	
ladylike	☐	
wavy hair	☐	
Negative actions		
be a thorn in the side of	☐	
betray	☐	
bring disgrace on	☐	
make fun of	☐	
insult	☐	
throw sb out	☐	
turn nasty	☐	
eject	☐	
Tools		
hammer	☐	
hatchet	☐	
chain	☐	
padlock	☐	
bolt clippers	☐	

Find out more

Branding and fundraising

The WSPU would not have been able to operate without money.

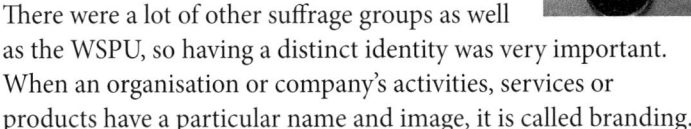

- Can you remember how they raised money for their campaigns?

There were a lot of other suffrage groups as well as the WSPU, so having a distinct identity was very important. When an organisation or company's activities, services or products have a particular name and image, it is called branding.

- What branding did the WSPU use?
- How did Sylvia Pankhurst and Emmeline Pethick-Lawrence create the WSPU branding?

WebQuest:

Go to Google Arts & Culture and look at Suffragette Branding by Museum of London: https://artsandculture.google.com/story/CgWBzd0nBe1UKQ?hl=en

- What examples of fundraising can you find?
- What branded items can you see?
- If you were a supporter of women's suffrage, would you buy any of the items? Why/why not?

On the same website you can learn about the Women's Exhibition the WSPU held in May 1909. Look at the images and information and answer these questions:

- Why did the WSPU hold the exhibition?
- When was it open to the public?
- How many stalls were there and what could you buy?
- What was the most popular stall and how much money did it make?
- How did the WSPU publicise the Exhibition?
- How many new members did they recruit?

Modern campaigning

In Chapter 1 you were asked to think about what social, environmental or political problems you are worried about at the moment.

Have a look online, on the internet and/or social media, for examples of different campaign groups you know of. If you have not heard of any campaign groups you could look at Fridays for Future, Extinction Rebellion, Just Stop Oil, Black Lives Matter, Womankind Worldwide or Centenary action.

Do you think any of the groups are similar to the WSPU in terms of:
• their cause
• the type of action they take
• how they raise money
• police action against them

Which group do you think has the best branding?

Create your own campaign

Now create an imaginary campaign group to fight for a cause you are interested in. Decide on the following:
• the name of your organisation
• a motto
• eye-catching branding (colours, a logo)
• how you will raise money
• how you will recruit members
• what type of action you will take e.g. marches, petitions
• how you will publicise your campaigns

The law-abiding suffragists

The WSPU was not the only organisation fighting for votes for women – there was also The National Union of Women's Suffrage Societies (NUWSS), whose leader was Millicent Garrett Fawcett. There were a lot of difference between both organisations. The

NUWSS was much larger - in 1914 it had over 100,000 members whereas the WSPU only had 2,000. The NUWSS was also non-violent and more democratic than the WSPU.

You can learn more about Millicent Garrett Fawcett here:
https://artsandculture.google.com/story/3QUxWhVBH8FaLw

Why do you think Emmeline Pankhurst is more famous than Millicent Garrett Fawcett?

Women in Parliament

Take a 360° virtual tour of the Houses of Parliament
https://www.parliament.uk/visiting/virtualtour/
Click on the tab for 'Women in Parliament' and visit the different places in the UK parliament. Read the information in the purple circles and find the answers to these questions:

Central Lobby How long were women banned from the Central Lobby?
House of Commons Chamber What did the Women's Freedom League do in 1908?
House of Lords Chamber When did Frederick Pethick-Lawrence become a member of the House of Lords?
Members' Lobby Apart from Keir Hardie, which other two men were important supporters of women's suffrage?
Peers' Lobby What did Lady Rhondda want to do?
St Stephen's Hall How long did it take to clean the wall after Marion Wallace-Dunlop had stamped the Bill of Rights extract on it?
Westminster Hall What did Sylvia Pankhurst ask Keir Hardie to do for her?

Look at the **timeline** from 1832 to 1979. Can you match the events you have learnt about in this book to any of the dates? Which ones did you get right?

Answer key

Before you start
1. d, 2. g, 3. k, 4. a, 5 e, 6. h, 7. b, 8. i, 9. f, 10. c

Introduction
1. On 15th July 1858 in Manchester, England. 2. There were
3 reforms acts which extended the vote to more men. 3. It started
in 1866 with the first mass petition signed by 1,500 women.
4. She went to her first suffrage meeting. 5. Because he was a
radical with left-wing political views. Red is the colour associated
with socialism or communism. 6. He drafted the Married Women's
Property Act, worked on women's suffrage court cases and was a
member of the Manchester National Society for Women's Suffrage.
7. In December 1879. 8. She had 5 children. 9. They controlled
the workhouse, where poor people could sleep and get food in
exchange for working. 10. She found a job as a registrar of births
and deaths in Manchester so she could look after her family.
11. They earned lower salaries than men, they paid for dinner
for poor children from their salaries and they didn't receive
much training. 12. The Women's Social and Political Union – it
campaigned to get the vote for women. 13. It was 'talked out' or
stopped from being successful because it was discussed for too long
and there was not enough time for it to go to the next stage.

Focus on the story
Questions at the end of each chapter

Chapter 1
- Emmeline's parents were supporters of women's suffrage and she first went to a suffrage meeting with her mother when she was 14. Her experience on the Board of Poor Law Guardians, the Manchester school board and as a registrar of births and deaths also convinced her that women needed to be able to vote.
- That the actions that you do (your deeds) are more important that what you say (your words).

Chapter 2
- They allowed the WSPU to use their house as its headquarters, they raised money and helped the organisation grow, they started and edited 'Votes for Women'.
- They used their newspaper, 'Votes for Women', they stood on chairs on the streets and rang hand bells and handed out pamphlets.

Chapter 3
- An old law that said it was illegal for anyone to take a petition to Parliament if they had more than 10 other people with them.
- Prisoners had to wear dirty prison clothes. The cells were small, dark and damp and they smelled bad, at night they were freezing and the bed was hard. In the first month prisoners were in solitary confinement, they could not speak to anyone or have visitors and had nothing to do. They only had an hour of exercise every day.

Chapter 4

- To show the government that women's suffrage had a lot of public support.
- So that when people saw the colours, they would immediately think about votes for women.

Chapter 5

- Because he thought all men should have the vote first and that women did not know enough about national politics. He also believed women would vote for the Conservative Party and the Liberals would lose political power.
- She wanted to be treated as a political prisoner and to be moved to the first division in prison.

Chapter 6

- Because the colour black is associated with darkness and bad things and on Black Friday the suffragettes were assaulted and humiliated by the police.
- Because peaceful demonstrations had not worked, and the government and police replied with violence. The destruction of property had also been a successful tactic used by men.

Chapter 7

- They became more violent. Some members did not agree with these actions and left the WSPU including Sylvia, Adela and the Pethick-Lawrences.
- A law that allowed hunger strikers to leave prison so they could recover their health, when they were better, they had to return to prison.

Focus on the story

1. 1. j, 2. e, 3. m, 4. b, 5. g, 6. o, 7. h, 8. a, 9. n, 10. k, 11. f, 12. c, 13. l, 14. i, 15. d

2. **Manchester** (example) - *Emmeline was born in Manchester. It's also important because it's where Annie Kenney and Christabel Pankhurst asked the Liberal Part about votes for women.* **Caxton Hall** was close to the Houses of Parliament and is where the WSPU had public suffrage meetings. **Parliament/ the House of Commons** is the home of the UK government. **Clement's Inn** was the home of the Pethick-Lawrences and the WSPU headquarters in London. **Holloway Prison** was the women's prison in London where the WSPU members who broke the law were sent. **Hyde Park** is where the Women's Sunday demonstration and 500,000 people attended. *10 Downing Street* is the home of the UK Prime Minister. **Paris** is where Christabel escaped to after the police raid on Clement's in 1912.

3. Incorrect options are: 1. c, 2. a & d, 3. b & c, 4. a, c & d, 5. a & c

Focus on the people

1. **Christabel:** 1, 4, 8, 13, 17 **Sylvia:** 3, 6, 12, 16, 19 **Emmeline Pethick-Lawrence:** 2, 7, 10, 15, 18 **Herbert Henry Asquith:** 5, 9, 11, 14, 20

2. 1. oldest, 2. favourite, 3. studied law, 4. is always true to the WSPU motto, 5. religious, 6. artistic, 7. socialist, 8. works with other political parties, 9. pacifist, 10. disgraces the Pankhurst family name, 11. wealthy, 12. excellent fundraiser, 13. edits the first WSPU newspaper, 14. efficient organiser, 15. doesn't believe the end justifies the means, 16. arch-enemy, 17. political reformer, 18. breaks his promise, 19. anti-suffragette, 20. WSPU target

3. Reader's own answer

4. 1. Adela, 2. Dr Richard Pankhurst, 3. Mary, 4. Dr Strode, 5. James Keir Hardie, 6. Richard, 7. Annie Kenney and Flora Drummond, 8. Mary Leigh and Edith New, 9. Marion Wallace Dunlop, 10. Emily Wilding Davison, 11. Herbert Gladstone and Reginald McKenna

Focus on grammar

Emmeline has been: a daughter, a wife, a mother of five children, a social reformer, a widow, a suffragette, a prisoner, a hunger striker and a thorn in the side of the Liberal government.

Past participles: 1. *been*, 2. broken, 3. brought. 4. came/became, 5. cost, 6. done, 7. eaten, 8. fought, 9. gone, 10. had, 11. heard, 12. hidden, 13. known, 14. left, 15. lost, 16. made, 17. seen, 18. taken, 19. told, 20. written

1. **For:** *30 minutes*, a quarter of an hour, several days, 30 years, a very long time, several months, as long as she can remember. **Since:** *half past ten*, 1900, the First World War, the morning, she was in prison, the King's Speech, the spring
2. a. 1. has fought, a. as long as she can remember, b. 2. haven't eaten/have not eaten, b. several days, c. 3. has had, c. she was in prison, d. 4. has been, d. the spring, e. 5. have known, e. a very long time
3. a. *Christabel has already announced the processions in 'Votes for Women'.* b. *WSPU members haven't distributed handbills around London yet.* c. Sylvia has already designed handbills and posters. d. Sylvia and Annie have already put up posters in shop windows. e. WSPU members haven't chalked announcements on pavements yet. f. Frederick has already booked trains into London. g. The Pankhurst sisters haven't made purple, white and green rosettes yet.

4. Qs: 1. How long have you lived in your current town or city? 2. Write down something that you have just learnt about Emmeline Pankhurst. 3. What other DELTA readers have you read so far? 4. Is there anything important that you haven't done today but you should have? 5. Have you finished all the questions in this activity yet?
As: Reader's own answers.

Build your vocabulary
Focus on words and phrases

1. 1. b a petition Why? *A petition is when a member of the public asks the government to do something, The others are connected to laws that the governments make.* 2. d House of Commons Why? The House of Commons is a place. The others are jobs in the government. 3. c a social reformer. Why? A social reformer is an occupation. The others are related to family. 4. a radical Why? A radical describes somebody who is in favour of complete political or social change. The others are types of police. 5. b assault Why? To assault sb means to attack sb physically. The others are related to fire. 6.c motto Why? A motto is a short sentence that says what an organisation believes. The others are ways of communicating printed on paper. 7. b ally Why? An ally is somebody who supports you. The other are people who are against you.

2. 1. banner, 2. fine, 3. march, 4. strengthen, 5. whisper, 6. bruise, 7. equality, 8. goal, 9. motto, 10. slogan, 11. suffrage, 12. filthy, 13. guilty, 14. nod, 15. starve

D	E	D	G	B	N	S	S	Y	T	S	R
H	O	S	X	O	L	O	T	Q	U	S	E
N	C	W	I	O	A	L	R	F	Y	T	N
U	C	R	G	U	I	L	F	E	H	R	N
F	E	A	A	U	R	R	U	Q	T	E	A
Z	N	Q	G	M	A	B	C	U	L	N	B
R	Q	B	W	G	I	R	A	A	I	G	D
W	X	C	E	D	J	R	X	L	F	T	E
E	V	R	A	T	S	I	C	I	P	H	P
E	W	H	I	S	P	E	R	T	L	E	U
I	E	N	I	F	D	V	C	Y	U	N	V
M	O	T	T	O	B	F	I	M	U	G	R

3. 1. home, 2. side, 3. out, 4. Speech, 5. clock, 6. rain, 7. flames, 8. ears, 9. solitary, 10. history

Find out more

Branding and fundraising

The WSPU raised money by charging to join the organisation, selling 'Votes for Women' and badges and pins. / WSPU branding included their motto 'Deeds, not words' and the white, purple and green colours. / Sylvia designed posters, badges and pins etc and Emmeline Pethick-Lawrence created the colours.

WebQuest

Examples of fundraising: garden parties, afternoon teas, bazaars and fairs, WSPU shops sold merchandise / Examples of branded items: motor scarf, badges, Christmas card, board game, tea set.

Women's Exhibition
It was held to raise funds, recruit members and publicise the campaign. / It was open May 13th-26th from 2.30 to 10:30pm every day. / There were 50 stalls and you could buy hats, dresses, flowers, produce, sweets and refreshments. / The refreshment stall was the most popular and it made £600. / They publicised the Exhibition with processions and performances by the Women's Drum and Fife Band. / They recruited 250 new members.

Women and Parliament
Central Lobby – women were banned for 11 years. / **House of Commons Chamber** – they hung a banner demanding votes for women from the Ladies Gallery **House of Lords Chamber** – Frederick Pethick-Lawrence became a member of the House of Lords in 1945 / **Members' Lobby** - John Stuart Mill and George Lansbury / **Peers' Lobby** – Lady Rhondda wanted to inherit her father's seat in the House of Lords. / **St Stephen's Hall** – It took over 2 hours to clean the wall. / **Westminster Hall** – Sylvia asked Keir Hardie to request a meeting between MPs and working-class women campaigning for the vote.
Events in this book on the **timeline** - 1832 Great Reform Act, 1866 first mass suffrage petition, 1897 NUWSS formed, 1803 WSPU formed, 1905 suffragette militancy, 1907 WFL formed, 1909 force feeding begins, 1913 Emily Wilding Davison dies, 1913 Cat and Mouse Act introduced, 1914 militant activity suspended & First World War, 1918 first women gain the vote, 1928 equal voting rights.

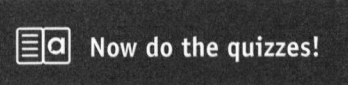 **Now do the quizzes!**